UNCONDITIONAL
LIBERATED BY LOVE

UNCONDITIONAL
LIBERATED BY LOVE

JESSE CUPP

Endorsements

The ministry of Jesus was straightforward, simple, and powerful to set people free and heal their lives. Jesse Cupp's message and ministry is very similar. He is a man on a mission, a mission to set the captives free and to invite people into a love encounter with the same God that set him free. In his book, *Unconditional: Liberated by Love*, the reader will have this same opportunity. Through powerful testimonies of God's loving intervention and impossible situations turned completely around, *Unconditional* will inspire you to hope and to walk into a fresh freedom that comes through encountering the person, Truth. I encourage you to pick up a copy of *Unconditional* and simply, powerfully receive the Father's blessing!

—Danny Silk
Senior Leader at Bethel Church, Redding, California
Senior Leader at Jesus Culture, Sacramento, California
Author of *Keep Your Love On* and *Culture of Honor*

Unconditional: Liberated by Love releases the good news of the gospel in an incredible, understandable, and practical way. Through Jesse's revelation of Scripture and the sharing of his personal struggles and victories, you will be ignited with hope and purpose through really knowing you are loved by the Father.

—Steve Backlund
Author, speaker, and beliefs coach with Igniting Hope Ministries

I personally know Jesse Cupp to be a genuine and powerful follower of Jesus, and that comes across in every chapter of this book. Jesse allows you a vulnerable look into his life and the valuable keys that have brought him into the intimate relationship with Jesus he walks in today.

This book is full of life-changing keys that will empower every reader to live a fuller, more intimate, and fruitful life in God. My sincere hope is that you allow the truths in this book to transform you into the intimate lover and powerful world-changer Jesus has called you to be.

—Joaquin Evans
Director of Bethel Activation Ministries, Bethel Church,
Redding, California.

Jesse has done a great job in *Unconditional: Liberated by Love*. In *Unconditional*, Jesse communicates the heart of God. This is a perfect book to pick up and read as a devotional, because it is packed with so many wonderful, relevant topics that the believer is asking questions about. Questions such as: *Does God love and accept me as I am? Does grace just save me, or can it transform me? How can I be a free and powerful Christian?* As you read this book, expect God to minister to your heart about how He sees you from the eyes of Love.

—Chris Overstreet
Outreach Director at Bethel Church, Redding, California
Author of *A Practical Guide to Evangelism – Supernaturally*

Jesse Cupp is happier in his own skin than most people I've met. The reason he is so comfortable with himself is wrapped up in his relationship with God through Jesus Christ. In this delightful read, he creates a roadmap to understanding your full identity as God created you. The entire book reeks of practical tools to disarm sin and condemnation while moving into a lifestyle of joy and freedom.

—Ralph Moore
Founder of the Hope Chapel Movement
www.ralphmoorehawaii.com

It gives me great pleasure to introduce you to a book, *Unconditional: Liberated by Love*, and the author Jesse Cupp. This book and the author have both personally touched my life and my heart. When Jesse asked me to write an endorsement for his book, my first thought was "Another book on love…." There are truly thousands, if not millions of songs, poems, and books written on love. However, there are few on the subject of unconditional love.

The book you are about to read is a mixture of God's truth, powerful testimonies, real-life honesty, and humility. Jesse takes us on a journey, through his eyes, of God's great grace. Jesse is a part of the B.A.M. (Bethel Activation Ministries) team. He has spent many hours ministering, encouraging, and loving on pastors and their churches while pursuing the unconditional love of the Father. I am grateful for Jesse and his investment in the Kingdom. His gifting has allowed him to operate as a strong leader with a soft touch. To say it another way, He is a powerful anointed tool in God's toolbox. He demonstrates the words you are about to read many times over.

The Bible says, "*Have any of these prophets been in the Lord's presence to hear what he is really saying?*" (Jeremiah 23:18). "*If they had stood before me and listened to me, they would have spoken my words, and they would have turned my people from their evil ways*" (Jeremiah 23:22).

Jesse's words truly come from him being in the Lord's presence. He is a man of integrity and his words speak truth into people's hearts.

—Doug Roe
Senior Pastor of Vineyard Church, Dayton, Ohio

I have read a lot of books about God and His love, but not one has blessed me like *Unconditional*. Its compassion, its "I've been there" tone, its accessibility, and its joyful invitation to a life with a loving God will bless your socks off. Jesse is the real deal, and his stories of his own journey and that of many of his close friends will challenge you to shed your fears of walking with the Lover of our souls. It's a book you won't want to put down, and you won't want far from your reach, *ever*. You will want to stay in the peaceful, joyful world it invites you to join. A must read!

—Dr. Todd Royse
Chiropractic First, Redding, California
www.chirofirst.net

Dedication

To Scott Cupp—my dad and my hero:

You are a greater man than you may ever know. Your courage, compassion, and passion for God planted seeds in us kids at an early age that have grown into well-watered trees. We have seen a great measure of the glory that God has stored within you, and we are eager to see it all unveil. I don't think you or I have seen anything yet compared to what is coming. I love you, appreciate you, and believe in you!

To all the believers out there who feel like you fall short of what the perfect Christian is:

You are more amazing than you know! How could you *not* be with Jesus Christ living inside of you? He chose *you*, not the other way around. Jesus is amazing in you, and He is transforming your outward experience into your inward reality, which is "*Christ in you, the hope of glory*" (Colossians 1:27). I believe in you; and more importantly, so does God!

Acknowledgements

Jessica:
Thank you for so sacrificially supporting me as I've spent countless hours working hard on writing my first book. You believe in me and my message. Your support has helped my dream come true. I love you!

Steve Backlund and Pam Spinosi:
Thank you for inspiring me, activating me, and cheering me on. You made me believe I can do this now instead of at some unforeseen later time.

Jessica Cupp, Katrina Stevenson, Link Tipton, Robb Burkee, David Jonas, and Rose Winn:
Thank you for selflessly giving your time and heart to give thoughtful and helpful feedback to me. Your input refined and upgraded this work significantly.

Chris Tracy, Dr. Todd Royse, and Angel Anan:
Thank you for taking the quality of this book to the next level. If it has any hint of professionalism, your magic touch helped tremendously.

Wes Ireton:
Thanks for a fantastic book cover and all your help.

Maureen Cutajar:
Thank you for formatting this book and making it more appealing to the reading eye.

Contents

Foreword

You have in your hands a great book. *Unconditional* is Jesse Cupp's story about the revelation he has personally received of God's unconditional love. He unlocks this powerful biblical truth for us and tells us how we can experience God's love for ourselves. With each chapter, Jesse keeps releasing more good news about identity in Christ and how God really sees us. "This is too good to be true!" may be your response. If so, then it means you are hearing the real gospel like never before, and you are being set up for radical freedom and joy as you abide in the Father's approval.

Jesse weaves his story throughout the book. As you hear of his struggles and victories in actions and beliefs, you will receive abounding hope for your life. *Unconditional* is not some lofty theological dissertation, but it is a practical journey into deep truth through Jesse's own experiences (which we can all relate to).

I have had the privilege of having Jesse as a part of my life during the past few years. He interned for me and continues to be a part of my ministry family. He is a man of sincerity, humility, and integrity. He is a releaser of the supernatural, a lover of his family, and a great strength to our movement and to me. He has experienced great highs in life and ministry, and he has gone through some very challenging circumstances. But whatever he has faced, I have found him to have his life well anchored in the truths of this book. I am proud of him for how he influences others in Christ, but I am more proud for how he lives his life.

As you read this book, get ready to be changed. Get ready to encounter God's unconditional love in dramatic ways. Get ready to believe God is good like never before. You are being set up for a glorious season in life, and this book holds many of the keys to enter into it.

Bless you much,

Steve Backlund
Author, Speaker, Beliefs Coach with Igniting Hope Ministries

Scars Don't Define You

The pain was unbearable. Top-heavy with anguish, she may have preferred lugging five bags of concrete in a backpack. Hopelessness was her worldview and loneliness her closest companion. I'll never forget the night I met amazing, beautiful, princess Catie!

It was September of 2011 and I was traveling with my mentor, Steve Backlund, being trained for itinerant revival ministry. We were in a small church right outside of Detroit, Michigan. Steve had just finished preaching. Standing in the front of the room, I was approached by Catie to receive prayer for healing. For four years, Catie had suffered from 20 ulcers in her esophagus and couldn't even swallow water without excruciating pain.

Just before I began to pray for her, she blurted out that she was also suffering depression. I was the first person she opened her heart to about the fact that two years prior, her fiancé committed suicide just 90 days before their wedding date. The tragedy hit an even lower low when she read in the suicide note that it was all her fault. He said she was the worst girlfriend and fiancé in the world. He left her with the "gift" of guilt. She felt so worthless and hopeless.

Once I learned of her horrific situation, I felt the best thing I could give her was an encounter with the Prince of Peace. Jesus was ready to heal a broken heart. When I invited God to touch her with His manifest love, His presence fell on her. Her soul was filled with the peace that surpasses understanding. She said that it felt like a million pounds had lifted off her shoulders. For the first time ever, Catie began to believe that it wasn't her fault.

After this amazing touch from God, I asked her how her esophagus was feeling. We had someone get her a bottle of water to test it out. She was terrified, but courageously took a drink. The pain was gone. Over the next few months, the ulcers completely disappeared and, to this day, haven't come back. God is so good! And with this new peace, for the first time in three years, she was able to sleep soundly without sleeping pills.

I had no idea that what she shared with me was only a sliver of the burden she was carrying. Three years earlier, Catie woke up one morning and found her mother dead from a heart attack on the living room couch. The last conversation they had together was a heated argument. Certain family members blamed the death on stress caused by Catie.

"You are nothing…. You aren't smart enough…. You aren't pretty enough." The first time she remembers hearing this was when she was four, and the declarations have never ceased. All her life, she was plagued with declarations by close family members that all the problems were always her fault and she would never amount to anything. Her grandfather was a church deacon who often told her, "You're going to hell."

When Catie was about 13, she learned a new coping mechanism. Bullied in school and at home, she needed a way to release her pain, so she began cutting herself on the forearms and wrists. By the time she was 16, she realized that it had become an addiction. If she didn't cut herself, she felt like she would explode. Some of the slashes were actual attempts at suicide.

Throughout Catie's life, she has suffered grief from the loss of more than 50 close loved ones. Many were from accidental drug overdoses; over half were from suicide. Their reasons included: they weren't good enough; they felt completely useless; there was no hope for things to change; they didn't believe they were worthy of anything good. She says that most had set standards for themselves that couldn't ever possibly be reached. These beliefs were common to how Catie felt about herself.

One Friday morning in June 2011, she woke up from her sleep and found herself on a hospital bed. Replaying through her mind her last memory, she understood that her plan failed. The night before, she intentionally overdosed on Xanax and other anti-depressants, hoping to end her misery. Lying in that sterile, white room, Catie began to realize that maybe she should try to figure out who she really was since trying to hide from her pains wasn't fixing the problem.

Two days later, her friend took her out for ice cream, or so she thought. She actually was tricking her into going to a young adults' church service. Five hundred people were there. Catie was upset with her friend for deceiving her; she didn't like church or crowds. But she was appeased with the $50 bribe that her friend promised her if she would sit through the entire service.

After the meeting was over, the pastor came and met her. He shared with her his testimony of God saving him from drugs while living on the streets of Detroit. It moved her heart to see that someone as broken as she could find hope in Christ. Catie gave her life to Jesus that night and began the journey to discover who she really was.

At the beginning of her Christian journey, she believed love couldn't be real unless there were conditions. She was so full of guilt and shame and thought that there was no way Jesus could love and forgive her. She was thankful for salvation but felt she still had to carry her own burdens and misery.

On the night I met her in September 2011, the Holy Spirit released the love of God upon her and something began to shift in her heart. When the million pound weight was lifted, she realized that maybe God really did love her just as she was. Perhaps His love really was unconditional. She got the revelation that God was not so complicated and His love was simple.

She used to believe hope didn't exist; but now she saw that hope also was simple. She began to see that she was not a failure and God actually had wonderful plans for her life. Her journey continued into an unveiling of her royalty in Christ, and she discovered that she was a princess to God despite any of the junk she was walking through.

Fast forward to April 2013. Catie was relentlessly pursuing God like a champion. One midweek day, she looked at all the scars she had cut into her arms. There were at least 75 scars per arm, totaling more than 150. Reflecting on how her life had radically transformed since the time when she would self-mutilate, she realized she was tired of this constant physical reminder of who she used to be. She said out loud, "I wish these stupid things didn't define me any longer!" She was tired of having to cover them up with long sleeves or makeup so people wouldn't judge her by her past.

That Saturday morning, she attended a worship service at a conference where Georgian Banov and Heidi Baker were the speakers. The congregation was singing *Oh, How He Loves Us*. Catie was in a bad mood that morning and grew irritated with how emotional everyone was in their expressions of worship. She was annoyed because she wanted to be free in her worship like they were. Halfway through the song, as she was about to head back to her seat from the front, she felt the presence of God come upon her.

She noticed her arms began tingling and burning. Pulling her sleeves back to see what was happening, she got the shock of her life. Some of her scars were gone! As she stared at them in awe, individual scars began glowing and then disappeared, one after another. What kind of miracle was this? The glory of God was resting on Catie as He was giving her a sloppy wet kiss from Heaven. She says she is not one to shake under the power of God, but she was this time. People nearby were staring at her strangely. She didn't care. She was watching every single scar that she carved into her arm in a former life disappear before her very eyes. All 150 vanished, leaving no traces of scar tissue.

"At first I didn't believe it. Scars can't go away. But all the guilt and the pain, the years of torment and the shame, they all went away with the scars," she said. She continued, "This was the first time I felt like all the excuses for why God couldn't love me were completely eliminated." As her outward appearance was being transformed, so was her heart. She was washed clean.

God agreed with Catie that those scars will never define her again. She is not the person she once was who would do such a thing. She is now redeemed as a beloved daughter of the Most High God.

Catie explained to me what she believes about herself now. "God loves me just for who I am, not for what I do. Now God reassures me that He loves me just simply because I am me. For the first time in my life, I don't feel guilty about anything. The past is behind me. All the bad things happened, but they are not who I am. I got the revelation that my identity is not in my failures and losses but in being a child of God." And she is living more freely than she ever has. Catie is one of my heroes in the faith.

(If you have not experienced a life-changing encounter with Jesus Christ as your Lord and Savior, this is your moment! He can transform your identity derived from past mistakes into that of a child of God. If you desire to receive this kind of salvation, which removes all guilt from your life and replaces it with love, joy, and peace, please wait no longer! Bookmark this page to return to later and quickly turn to the Appendix in the back of this book. Read the section called *Meet the Lover of Your Soul*. The remainder of this book is written to born-again Christians. It's time for you to discover the unconditional love of God for yourself. You will not regret it!)

2

Trumped by the Cross

What is the difference between a bad haircut and a good haircut? About two weeks. That was a joke that would have probably been funnier had I heard it from a friend or on a sitcom. But I heard it from a stylist who was cutting my hair! I had never met her before and had no grid for what she was thinking. Was she trying to practice comedy? Or was she trying to pad a safe pathway from my chair to the cash register after a wrong snip? In faith, I granted her a nervous courtesy laugh.

There's nothing like a bad haircut. First, you don't feel good about yourself. And more so, you are self-conscious that every person on the planet has a close-up view of the hedge work your budget hairstylist hacked out. Well, at least that's been my experience more than once. (Please, no offense to anyone who works at one of these places or gets serviced by them. I've been a loyal patron for most of my life. I'm just venting.) I don't like leaving the salon looking like Jim Carrey in *Dumb and Dumber* or having to touch it up myself at home.

One time, my friend, Joni (a professional hairstylist), informed me that the hair shops I go to are the McDonald's of salons. I guess sometimes I have left feeling the same as if I were dining with my flashy-fashioned friends at a fancy restaurant while eating a Happy Meal and wearing a fanny pack. When the stylist doesn't get it right, it just doesn't make me feel super good about myself.

Condemnation is like a bad haircut. You don't feel good about yourself, and it seems like everybody around can see every flaw on you. But

9

the other thing they both have in common is that it's something some-one else put on you; neither one is who you really are.

This provokes two questions: Who puts condemnation on you? And who are you really?

It is a spirit of religion who tells you that your identity comes from what you do or don't do. And it is a spirit of condemnation that reminds you of the perpetual distance between your latest action and your desired destiny. It tells you that your character has just shifted from good to bad because you made a bad choice. It slaps shame on your head, and slime oozes down until it coats your entire being with the muck of unworthi-ness. It does all it can to convince you to believe that you are prone to the behaviors you committed when you sinned.

Condemnation, in the biblical sense, is a sentence to guilt and judgment. It comes as a form of false humility that makes you want to punish yourself for imperfection. The source of condemnation is not from Heaven. It is from hell. It is this attribute of false religion that pushes you to get rid of your sin on your own in order to be worthy to stand before God.

(My references to religion are targeted to ideals that we can gain favor with God by adhering to a set of institutionalized or self-inflicted rules, which tend to focus more on duty and performance than on relationship with God. This form of devotion to God is usu-ally inclined to fix its attention more on the failure to live up to standards and to leave one feeling unworthy of approval.)

Conversely, grace invites you to stand worthy before God just as you are. The cleansing of your sin simply happens as a natural by-product of His presence as you yield your heart to His. His throne is called the mercy seat; and it is in His presence where we are invited to come with boldness in order to receive mercy and the cleansing of our sin. (See Hebrews 4:15-16 and 10:19-22. This will be discussed in detail in later chapters.)

It is true that God does not delight in sin. He hates it, and He ex-pects purity from us. However, God has given us all we need to live in purity and holiness. He is not looking to punish us. He has actually already punished sin on the cross once and for all. God's response to our wrongdoing is not anger and punishment; it is absolute love. *"There is no fear in love; but perfect love casts out fear, because fear involves punishment, and the one who fears is not perfected in love"* (1 John 4:18). He may at times see the need to bring discipline to us in order to lead us into repentance, as repentance is a vital part of our reconnection with Him. But this is an act of His love, which longs for a restoration of intimacy (see 2 Corinthians 7:9-11).

Religion's response to sin is condemnation, which is fear-based. God's response to sin is grace, which is love-based. Neither one can work with the other. It's like oil and water. And we get to choose from which source we prefer to quench our thirsty souls.

I believe one of the major forces that causes us to miss out on the glory of God is the belief that we must be punished for our sins. It is too easy to retain a lasting feeling of guilt and unworthiness, even after heartfelt confession to God. I used to believe sin was the thing that kept us separate from the glory of God. After all, Romans 3:23 says, *"For all have sinned and fall short of the glory of God."*

I have spent a large part of my walk with God focusing on all of my weaknesses. I lived a revolving cycle of joyful confidence and shameful unworthiness, all based on how much or how little time I could keep myself abstaining from the temptations of sin. My return to confident faith after I sinned would be based on how "hard" I repented and how long it had been since I committed the sin. After all, doesn't there have to be a probationary period restricting us from the Courts of the Holies? I used to believe so.

On the contrary, sin which is surrendered to God in repentant faith has completely lost its power to separate us from our connection with Him. In spite of sinning and falling short of the glory, Paul proceeds to regard us who believe (the same ones who sinned and fell short of the glory) as *"being justified* (made righteous) *as a gift by His grace through the redemption which is in Christ Jesus"* (Romans 3:24). The cross became the game changer we all needed. We are no longer under the Old Covenant that had its primary focus on sin and behaviors. Now it isn't so much the fact that we've sinned, but how we believe that can cause us to miss the glory.

What I mean is this: how we handle the sin we've committed and what we believe about ourselves after the fact are the determinants of whether or not we will find our way back into His glorious presence. No doubt that willfully choosing sin in our hearts over God is probably choosing an exit door from our experiential connection with His abiding glory. But what about the heart that truly doesn't desire to remain infected with sin?

We will discuss this issue of dealing with sin in a later chapter. However, a more critical matter is the issue of knowing our identity. What defines who you are? It is impossible to properly deal with sin if we don't first understand who we really are.

Linked to Jesus' Profile

When I was around four years old, every time Sunday School was over, Mom and Dad would ask me what I learned about in class that day. My answer was always thorough and thought-provoking. "Jesus," I would reply, the ever-safe answer. But before I could even get up the stairs to find my parents, my elderly Uncle Leonard, who was a church deacon, would come find me to swap a piece of pocket candy for a hug. One day he asked me how Sunday School was. I answered with sheer transparency, "Well, I didn't cuss." That must have been a victorious day of breakthrough for me!

It is a common tendency to believe Christianity is all about how much right and how little wrong we are doing. This is a sadly misleading perspective in the modern church. If we get our identity from what we are doing or how good we are doing it, we're going to be bipolar believers drawing strength only when we're on top of our mountains. But when the going gets tough, it's tougher to find security because we are anchoring it on our own abilities rather than on the Rock that never moves. If you fasten a mountain climbing rope only to yourself and not also to the anchors burrowed into the rock wall, as soon as you reach for a loose stone, you will be falling with nothing to save you. In the same way, faith is only beneficial when you place it in something stronger than yourself.

So here's the deal: **your sin is not God's primary focus!** It *was* one of His primary focuses, but Jesus took care of our problem. As a matter of fact, He dealt it a deadly blow. It is true that the wages of sin is death and the gift of God is eternal life. And with sin, we all deserved death. We all deserve eternal punishment and the wrath of God because all have sinned and fallen short of the glory of God. But the amazing Good News is that Jesus became our substitute and absorbed the wrath of God upon Himself so we wouldn't have to suffer it ourselves. Our sin has been trumped by the cross.

It was the ultimate sacrifice of love. He took our sins upon Himself and received the full punishment of all sin for all time. Jesus died in our place. God's wrath was fully satisfied on the cross of Christ for all who believe.

Do you know what is so amazing about what Jesus did on Calvary? It's not just that He took our sins upon the cross. Jesus had a whole lot more in mind there than simply rescuing us from the impending doom our recurring failures had been storing up for us. He went all the way. He took the very root source of our sins upon His bleeding, torn up carnage while hanging on that crossbeam. For everyone who believes, Jesus received our actual **sinful natures** onto the cross and **crucified them to death**.

> *Knowing this, that our old self was crucified with Him, in order that our body of sin might be done away with, so that we would no longer be slaves to sin; for he who has died is freed from sin* (Romans 6:6-7).

How could our old selves have been crucified with Christ? That was 2000 years ago, and I am certain I've never hung on a cross, not even in an Easter play. But there is a realm that makes no sense to the natural mind, and more happens there than meets the eye. Somehow, in the spirit via our faith, God has taken the invisible, interior part of who we are and joined it together with Christ in a timeless zone where the cross eternally resides.

"*In that day you will know that I am in My Father, and you in Me, and I in you,*" Jesus said in John 14:20. It is amazing to think about the mystery of how Christ could be *in me* and I could be *in Christ*. There are many scriptures that use these phrases. I don't know how to make sense of it except that Jesus says we are "one" with Him. This union with Christ affects us on so many levels, but it all begins at the cross. "...*We have become united with Him in the likeness of His death...*" (Romans 6:5).

We have been spliced into the awesome wonders that Jesus performed on that first Easter weekend. The complete gamut of the death, burial, and resurrection belongs to us. "*Therefore we have been **buried with Him** through baptism into **death**, so that as Christ was **raised from the dead** through the glory of the Father, so **we too might walk in newness of life**. For if we have become united with Him **in the likeness of His death**, certainly we shall also be **in the likeness of His resurrection**" (Romans 6:4-5).

If you want the full gospel, it has to include Jesus in His death, burial, and resurrection. But it also must include you and me, for we are in Christ. Our old man, who once drove us to inherently produce the fruit of sin, had its funeral with Him. Everything changed radically once we became "born again of the Spirit" (see John 3:1-8). Just as Jesus was called the *firstborn from the dead* after He was resurrected (see Colossians 1:18), we too were born anew from the dead. We passed from death in the kingdom of darkness to life in the Kingdom of Light. We became born again through the womb of the tomb. Our rebirth was literally a resurrection in Christ.

"*Reckon yourselves to be dead indeed to sin, but alive to God in Christ Jesus our Lord... present yourselves to God as being alive from the dead*" (Romans 6:11, 13 NKJV). We may not feel like we have died to the old man and been resurrected to newness of life in Christ. However, we must proactively train our minds and hearts to believe (to reckon) this and to live accordingly, in spite of how we feel or what our experiences tell us. Here is a truth to chew on: **your spirit is in union with the resurrected, glorified Christ!** And He wants you to draw life from this reality.

We were born into the family of God where we can rightfully call Him "Papa" or "Daddy." We aren't the same people we once were. "*If anyone is in Christ, he is a new creation; old things have passed away; behold, all things have become new*" (2 Corinthians 5:17 NKJV). Our new natures can no longer be associated with the things that have already been done away with. Sin has lost its power in our lives. Now we are free children of God.

Our union with Christ connects us with the transformation from death to life. Furthermore, we remain united with Christ even in His reinstatement back to His throne in Heaven. It was 40 days after His resurrection that the disciples witnessed the ascension of Jesus into the sky before He disappeared into the clouds (see Acts 1:9). He was elevated above all principality, power, might, and dominion and was seated at the right hand of the Father (see Ephesians 1:20-21).

Many years later, Paul prayed for the saints of God to be able to understand that the same power that worked in Christ is available for us who believe. He described this as the same power which raised Jesus from the dead, ascended Him above all other powers, and seated Him at the right hand of the Father in Heaven (see Ephesians 1:18-22).

Paul continued to describe the results of our union with Christ as this power is activated in us who believe.

"*Even when we were dead in our transgressions,* (God) **made us alive together with Christ...**"—this is the power of *resurrection.*

"*...and **raised us up with Him**...*"—this is the power of *ascension.*

"*... and **seated us with Him** in the heavenly places in Christ Jesus*" (Ephesians 2:5-6)—this is the power of *enthronement.*

Enthronement?

This means that we have been given a seat with Jesus Christ on His very throne in the heavenly places! This is our rightful place and position in the Lord, and it is the abode where our identity lies. You see, we live in Christ and He lives in us. "*I have been crucified with Christ; and **it is no longer I who live, but Christ lives in me**" (Gala-tians 2:20). And we get to sit with Him in the heavenly places at the right hand of Yahweh (God). Why? Because we are in Christ and He is in us.

"*Therefore if you have been raised up with Christ, keep seeking the things above, where Christ is, seated at the right hand of God*" (Colos-sians 3:1). If we truly desire to see and experience the glory of God, condemnation cannot have any room for influence. The devil, the world, and old, poor mindsets can cause us to miss out on spiritual realities that are far superior to our earthly experiences. We must lift our eyes above the circumstances that vie for our attention and fix them onto the truth that we are already seated at the right hand of God. So when the scripture says to "*set your mind on the things above, not on the things that are on earth*" (Colossians 3:2), it is actually calling on us to take our seat in the heavenlies and live in the reality of who the One sitting to our left thinks we are.

The fact is we cannot rely on our feelings if we want to live in the freedom provided to the born-again Christian. Feelings can be deceiving as we live in a world controlled by a spirit that lies to us continually about who we are, how good we are, and from where our strength is derived. What we must rely on is a faith that believes what God says about us and how good He has made us through the precious blood of Jesus. He has truly made us free; and He is the only one with the authority to tell us who we really are. So that is where we are heading to next...

The Journey of Self-Discovery

One of my former pastors, Bobby Jeter, was talking to a hitch-hiking hippy one time about his travels across the expanse of the great United States. He asked the wanderer what the purpose of his journey was. The young guy replied, "Hey man, I am just trying to find myself." Bobby looked deep in his eyes with compassion and hidden pleasure and said, "I have the answer to your mystery." He stuck his finger in his chest and said, "You are right there."

Who we are has nothing to do with job position, salary bracket, intelligence, abilities, hobbies, economic and social status, credit report, successes and failures, health condition, emotional cycles, or police records. These may be the things the systems of the world investigate when they "I.D." us. But our authentic identity comes from our Daddy in Heaven.

Now, I'll admit that it is unnatural for this fallen world to edify us or affirm the idea that we are seated in the heavenly places. Based on past experiences or the words of people that damn our mistakes louder than they applaud our successes, it can be difficult to believe that we are sons and daughters of the Most High God. Many of us may not have trouble believing we're children of God. However, we may have trouble believing that we are princes and princesses. But isn't that what a son and daughter of a king are? And don't they have full access to the royal palace?

If we are going to acknowledge that we have been born again, we must understand to Whom we have been born. From the womb of the tomb, our spirits passed through a channel that led us out of a life of hopeless bondage and into an open and eternal world, a domain of peace with our Maker. This was our rebirth. We have been held in the gentle hands of a loving Father ever since, being molded and crafted into His image.

God knows who we are, and we would do well to take His word for it. If we will believe what He is saying above how we are feeling, we will find ourselves being transformed more into His image. His word serves as a mirror to reveal to us how we carry His glory within us (see 2 Corinthians 3:18 and James 1:22-25).

My Identity Crisis

At some point we all must face an identity crisis of some sort. I would say I have probably faced a few throughout my life. I remember back in the not-so-glorious prepubescent years of junior high and early high school. I was trying so hard to climb my way up the popularity ladder. Imagine an uncoordinated pipsqueak trying to get the attention of the preppy jocks who were already shaving beards while I hadn't yet sprouted a single weed on my pits. I felt lucky that some of the studs actually had a heart to talk to me at times.

It was the popular thing in my school at that time to have a mullet on the back and sideburns shaved about an inch above the ears. I remember tagging along with some of the cool guys and would ask them if they think I should shave my sideburns like them. I must have looked like Napoleon Dynamite jealously asking Pedro if he thinks he should grow a mustache, even though he knew he couldn't. My self-confidence most certainly came from the affirmation I got from the people I admired. And that's why I had somewhere between little to none.

I was diligent in my venture to fame. I didn't stand much chance for status promotion due to a lack of great athletic skills. But I found a loophole, and it was one where I could hold my own. Comedy. That was one God-given talent I had inherited in my genetics that couldn't be taken away. I could make the best of them laugh. I had a true virtue that made people like who I was.

But I had a problem. It was in the way I perverted that gift for selfish gain. I believed the only way to ascend to new levels of popularity was at the expense of other people, causing them to descend into new levels of humiliation as I made fun of them. The more people I could shove under my feet, the more elevation I thought I would gain.

This seemed to work for a season. Rather than being content with who I was and the genuine joy I brought people, I was feeding off the sinister laughs my "superiors" gave me on loan. I sold my soul to the spirit of the world, which only promised acceptance to a falsified persona. Stepping onto a higher rung that was resting on someone else's head, I reached up for the next in thirst for another sip of self-glory. All the while, I was destroying reputations of the innocent and their sense of self-worth. I had forgotten from where I had come.

Although I was enjoying myself, I had no warning that I had already reached the highest peak of this mountain. I finally had a greater sense of self-worth and was building an identity I thought I could soon accept. But I hadn't built a structure that would be able to sustain me through a storm. Apparently this summit was made of sand. I didn't know that *pride goes before destruction, and a haughty spirit before stumbling*" (Proverbs 16:18).

Just as quickly as I initially contemplated climbing that ladder of popularity was how quickly I was shaken off of it. One day I was eating at the popular table in the center of the cafeteria; the next day I was scarfing my half-chewed food down at an empty table beside the exit, waiting to make a break for it.

Just minutes prior to this status exchange, I was in line having a good time with my friends. All of a sudden, one of the guys whose approval I was always striving to win shouted out a vulgar obscenity. It wasn't addressed to anyone obvious. The room quickly hushed to silence. I turned toward his audacious outcry. In slow motion, I instantaneously processed through a complete transition from laughter with the crowd in pleasure of the vulgarity to feeling an invisible dagger piercing through my ribcage. I could feel it wobbling in vibrations as it stuck me in the back. I realized I was the target for this slander, and it hit the bull's-eye in my heart.

For the rest of my freshman year, my crippled ego was eating alone and trying to hide from my new enemies who introduced me to the pain I had inflicted upon others more innocent than I. Within three days, the word spread and the entire school, it seemed, hated me and condemned me as a "faggot." I was not gay, but they bullied me with the same inhumane cruelty many gays have to suffer. My image had abruptly deteriorated from one fallacy to another.

From that day onward, I had to live life looking over my shoulders and trying to navigate a route in the shadows hoping to bypass the masses of bullies. I was now getting all the attention I could ever dream of, just not in the manner I wanted. Shoved around. Getting tripped. Books knocked out of hands. Books kicked like a soccer ball by students rushing to class. Barely dodging swirlies in filthy toilets. Close calls to getting beat up by people twice my size. Continually mocked and harassed. Welcome to my new freshman life.

I dreaded riding the bus because of the cruel students who promised a pulverizing. I also hated it because I arrived at school 45 minutes before class, leaving me helpless and vulnerable amongst the wolves with no adult to supervise. I found myself rushing to hide out in the computer lab with all the other rejects who found solace from the ravaging outside world. It was a refuge. I was now among the people I once enjoyed putting in this place.

Where was my identity now? It betrayed me because it had failed in its promises to give me the world and the riches of self-glory. Instead, it had returned to me a cheap ceramic mask, shattered to small pieces. And I didn't even need a broom because everyone around generously swept me up under the rug of despair. This was an identity crisis.

But it was being forced into this place of humility that I found myself desperately needing someone to love me for who I really was. Jesus knew He could finally get my attention, as He had been patiently waiting for this moment.

I would have attributed the pain and weakness I had crawled through as from the pits of hell. But I had no idea that it was by the mercy of God that I reaped what I had sown. In my cold biology class one day, as I was practicing my miserable coping mechanism of laying down my head to escape reality and enter Fantasy Land, my life was about to change.

I wouldn't have expected Jesus to visit Fantasy Land; but there He was, standing before me as if He were already strangely familiar with this imaginary world. Jesus. Gentle, strong, friendly Jesus. I felt His peace. I saw His glory. I sensed His love. I ignorantly had entered into a trance that brought me into a full-on vision of Jesus. I had thought a lot about Him in times past, but I never saw Him this up close and personal.

I felt as if He knew everything about me: all of my secret thoughts, my innermost desires, my lusts, my mercies, my false exterior contrasting my true inner self, my broken heart, and my feelings of fear, rejection, and abandonment. Yet with my naked soul exposed to both Him and myself in true form for the first time ever, He still cared.

His eternal eyes were full of tears and His strong yet gentle hands were full of warmth, embracing my shoulders. His eyes pierced my soul as He flooded my heart with true love and genuine words of affirmation, the kind that impart courage. He said to me, "I will never leave you nor forsake you, no matter what. I am a Friend who will stick closer than a brother." I didn't even know those were scriptures in the Bible (see Deuteronomy 31:6 and Proverbs 18:24).

This was the beginning of learning who Jesus really is to me and the slow journey of discovering who I am to Him. It has stripped my purposes and goals in life down to one: **to do everything I do out of intimacy with God**. This is where I feel complete. When I am at peace with God, I am at peace with myself. And this happens because I know that God is at peace with me, and I can't do anything to change that. His love will never change for me. I am accepted, no matter what.

Although part of my healing included moving to a different school district to be with my Christian friends, my deepest healing came when I realized that I am loved just as I am. The God of Heaven and Earth loves me more than I will ever know, and I am helpless to alter that. The Lord used my traumatic situation as a turning point, which brought my misguided eyesight into focus of a gravitational love that I still haven't been able to shake.

God is looking for a heart He can work with, one that is honest with Him and with self. This is the kind that He trusts with the greater riches of Heaven. Thankfully, as I discovered that real self-confidence is derived from confidence in God, my reputation was restored and has graced me with a bounty of lasting friendships. It is God who pronounces, affirms, and blesses our identity. Until we fully understand who He says we are, we are all going through some measure of an identity crisis.

Jesus' Identity

When Jesus was baptized in water by His cousin, John the Baptist, He also received from Heaven a greater baptism in the Holy Spirit. This empowered Him to begin His miracle ministry. Promptly after, the Holy Spirit led Him into the wilderness for a time of temptation by the devil. Matthew 4:2-3 says, "*And after He had fasted forty days and forty nights, He then became hungry. And the tempter came and said to Him, 'If You are the Son of God, command that these stones become bread.'*" The devil really knows how to bring his crafty work right at the most vulnerable of times.

I always thought the great sin Jesus was tempted with was to use His miracle powers for violating the laws of nature so He could sneak in some food on a fast. Was his goal to get Jesus to break early from a 40-day fast? I always thought so. But the text says it was *after* Jesus had fasted 40 days and 40 nights that He *then* became hungry. It wasn't until after Jesus had finished His fast that the devil began buttering Him up with the concept of a brick-oven bakery. Jesus was already free to eat at this point, so eating was not even a problem.

If the issue wasn't about breaking a fast, was the temptation about mutating the elements? Perhaps. But that wouldn't make sense either because, very soon, His inaugural miracle would be turning water into wine. So we can rule out both of these hypotheses about what was the basis of the temptation.

Let's have a further look at the story. Satan said to Him, *"If You are the Son of God, command that these stones become bread."* Jesus replied, *"It is written, man shall not live on bread alone, but on every word that proceeds out of the mouth of God"* (Matthew 4:4).

Notice that Jesus is not denying His right to eat bread, because that is not the issue, and neither is performance of any kind. But the devil would have it appear that way. He has cunning ways of hiding his deeper traps behind the decoys of superficial struggles. He will distract us with inferior external battles to lure our attention away from the deeper-rooted issues of the heart. He is waiting to pounce upon the unguarded heart so he can take it captive, while the naive diligently try to master outward performances.

Jesus was very discerning and saw right through the devil's ploy to lure Him into problems greater than what were visible to the naked eye. He knew very well that the scheme had nothing to do with bread. He actually exposed what truly was on trial: man lives *"on every word that proceeds out of the mouth of God."* He was being tested on whether or not He could be shaken from the Word of God. He specifically said that man lives on every *rhema* (Greek for this use of "word") that proceeds from the mouth of God.

Rhema refers to the right-now, revelatory word that is currently being uttered from God's mouth directly into your heart. Fresh revelation brings vibrant, abundant life to whoever will hear it and give it room to fill the heart and grow. Once *rhema* comes in, you own that word and it becomes a living substance from God where you can always find life as you ponder, guard, and steward it. *"The secret things belong to the LORD our God, but the things revealed belong to us and to our sons forever, that we may observe all the words of this law"* (Deuteronomy 29:29). The revealed word empowers you to be and do what it says of you.

What was the life-giving *rhema* Word that Jesus would not budge from? Let's look back to the most recent recorded word that proceeded from the mouth of God.

Forty days and one chapter earlier, Jesus was standing in the Jordan River with His cousin, John the Baptist. *"After being baptized,*

Jesus came up immediately from the water; and behold, the heavens were opened, and He saw the Spirit of God descending as a dove and lighting on Him" (Matthew 3:16). And His Father in Heaven pronounced over Him, *"This is My beloved Son, in whom I am well-pleased"* (Matthew 3:17).

Jesus was already known by many as a great man. He was already an excellent teacher of the law. Mary knew that He was the promised Messiah, but not many knew this yet. Surely Jesus did. But on this day, it was officially decreed over Him with an audible declaration from Heaven. This was a *rhema* Word from where Jesus would draw life.

God pronounced, affirmed, and blessed Jesus with a solid identity—that He was God's beloved Son, in whom He was well-pleased! This is who Jesus *was* and *is*. Just as enduring as God saying, "Let there be light" and there was light (that, might I add, has never stopped expanding), now God has spoken Jesus' identity, and it will never cease. Nothing can take it away from Him. The divine decree established it and sealed it in His heart. Jesus was confident in who He was. If God said it, it must be true.

In reading the entire context of this wilderness story, you can see that, in essence, Jesus' response to satan was saying, "Whoa! You just lost me at, '*If* You are the Son of God.' If God said it, it is. *I AM* His beloved Son, in whom He is well-pleased!"

The devil was trying to offend Jesus into self-defense by questioning His true identity. He wanted to subtly provoke Jesus into feeling the need to prove Himself. If Jesus had taken the bait to turn stones into bread, He would have been doing it to prove that He really was the Son of God. Perhaps satan's goal was to get Jesus to show off in pride in order to cause Him to fall (see Proverbs 16:18). If Jesus was trying to prove that to Himself, He would have been acting from doubt because He needed evidence that what God had spoken was true. Either way, the response would have separated Jesus from His true identity because of insecurity. Believing in our true identity always induces security.

It was a literal temptation for Jesus to feel the need to prove who He was. That means He must have actually considered it as an option.

There were many other times when Jesus faced this temptation. For example, people mocked Jesus saying, *"If you are the Son of God, come down from the cross"* (Matthew 27:40). Other times people tried to get Him to prove Himself by showing them a sign. He never felt the need to give in to this temptation. People who constantly think they need to prove themselves are actually proving their lack of confidence in their capabilities or character.

The battle between Jesus and satan was over His identity. Satan wanted to get Jesus to doubt who He was. If Jesus doubted who He was, then He would wane in His ability to achieve His purposes on Earth and His destiny to enter into the glory that awaited Him. If He would believe that He was anything less than the Son of God, He could not have possibly born the weight of the world on His shoulders. Even Jesus was facing a challenge to His identity that needed to be overcome.

But, glory to God, Jesus won the battle over His identity! He knew He didn't need to accomplish anything to attain to the stature He desired to have in God's eyes. It was already done and it wasn't hinged on performance or lack thereof. God was pleased with Jesus simply because He was His Son. Jesus had complete security in who He was and never allowed it to be shaken. He was rooted and grounded in the love of God. God said it, and that was good enough for Jesus. His faith didn't require proof because He took God's word at face value.

Although Jesus could smell the enticing fragrance of the luscious fruit on the wrong tree, He didn't flinch under pressure. He was not impatient to see God's glory revealed in Him through miracles. Jesus would have been just as secure if He never performed a miracle in His entire life. He would have been just as happy in His relationship with God if He never had crowds swarming Him in praise and adoration. He chose God's guidance and truth, often at the expense of disapproval by His greatest fans. He didn't need outward assistance to secure His inward identity. He truly knew who He was and was satisfied wholly by God's pleasure in Him rather than by momentary self-gratification.

Our Role Model

Jesus is our greatest role model. Maybe you have found it difficult to believe that God smiles upon you, perhaps because your circumstances don't feel like His pleasure. Or perhaps you don't feel secure in who you are as a son or daughter of God. But as Jesus found the way to victory in the battle over His identity, we must follow His lead. We must live by every word that proceeds out of the mouth of God, regardless of who our circumstances or others say we are.

It is time to believe at face value what God is saying about who we are to Him. He is saying the same thing over you and me as He said over Jesus Christ. "**You are My beloved child, in whom I am well-pleased!**" His pleasure in us is not based on our behaviors or performances; it is based on our sonship or daughterhood. He is so proud of you, and you can't change that!

5

Children of the Most High

When I was a kid, we had a dog named Monroe. He was just a little black mutt with a white patch on his chest. There was nothing special about him from the outside, but he had heart. He thought he was part of the family; and he was. But he literally thought he was our sibling born to Mom and Dad. It didn't take him long to become too good for Gravy Train. We even fed that guy "dog ice cream," but Monroe eventually turned his nose up to that, too. Why? Because someone started feeding him table scraps, even real ice cream at times, and he learned what he had been missing. Monroe would have sat at the head of the table to eat from a china plate with silverware if we had let him. But we did have *some* boundaries. He often became depressed when we sent him away from the dinner table while we were eating. It was his reminder that he truly was just our dog.

I am happy to tell you that neither you nor I are looked upon as the family dog in God's eyes! Things are different now than when the Gentile woman begged Jesus to deliver her daughter and He said, "*It is not good to take the children's bread and throw it to the dogs*" (Matthew 15:26). When Jesus went to the cross and performed His greatest miracle through the resurrection, He did it to elevate us from "dog-under-the-picnic-table" status to "children-at-the-banqueting-table" status. We are not orphan children who have been taken in as foster kids by a half-hearted, Good Samaritan God. We are not God's step-kids with a stepbrother named Jesus who tries to remind us we are only half-breeds. We have literally been born into the blood family of God and

29

are as equally His legitimate children as Jesus Christ Himself. In Christ, we have been adopted; but furthermore, we have been born again.

It was a big deal when God pronounced over Jesus that He was His beloved Son in whom He was well-pleased. He was revealing to the world exactly who Jesus was.

Colossians 1:15 says, "*He is the image of the invisible God, the firstborn of all creation.*" If Jesus was the firstborn, then it means there were others born of God after Him. That includes you and me! Jesus told Nicodemus that "*unless one is born again he cannot see the kingdom of God*" (John 3:3). We have "*been born again not of seed which is perishable but imperishable, that is, through the living and enduring word of God*" (1 Peter 1:23). We have been born again in spirit, and the Creator of the universe is our Daddy, just the same as He is to Jesus. His name is Yahweh. He has spoken this enduring word over us, and it is an imperishable promise.

He gave us His blood, not only redeeming us from the corruption of sin, but also bestowing to us His DNA. We are, in effect, children of a divine nature. "*For by these He has granted to us His precious and magnificent promises, so that by them you may become partakers* (partners) *of the divine nature…*" (2 Peter 1:4).

Romans 8:29 says, "*For those whom He foreknew, He also predestined to become conformed to the image of His Son, so that He would be the firstborn among many brethren.*" If God has predestined us to be conformed into the image of Jesus, and He is the image of the invisible God (Colossians 1:15), then that means God has chosen to imprint His image into us.

We already knew this though, didn't we? When God created man, He said, "*Let Us make man in Our image, according to Our likeness*" (Genesis 1:26). You and I were created in the image of God. So why then do we have the tendency to follow after Adam and Eve's mistake? That same old crafty snake Jesus dealt with came also to them in the garden to tempt them into eating from the forbidden tree. He coerced, "*God knows that in the day you eat from it your eyes will be opened, and you will be like God, knowing good and evil*" (Genesis 3:5).

Somehow in the heat of the moment of counterfeit bliss, they allowed satan's words to drown out the word which God had spoken over them. They became deceived and actually believed they needed to *do something* in order to become like God. To become like something essentially means that it is a separate entity which is identical to the other. In trying to become equal to God, they had to detach in order to attempt to match. But God had already created them in His image. They were one with Him...that is, up until this sad point of disconnection and self-achievement.

Thankfully, we are under a New Covenant by which Jesus has redeemed (purchased at full price and restored) us back to the state of the union God always intended for mankind. Now through Jesus Christ and His free gift of grace, we have been reconciled back to God. We are not separated but unified with Him again. It is to our detriment to think we need to do something to become like God in nature. He has already done it all in us, and we can just rest in who we are: God's kids.

Demoniac's Testimony

One day, Jesus and His disciples had crossed the sea and entered into the country of the Gerasenes. They parked the boat near a cemetery. There was a violent, demon-possessed man living there in torment. *"Seeing Jesus from a distance, he ran up and bowed down before Him; and shouting with a loud voice, he said, 'What business do we have with each other, Jesus, Son of the Most High God? I implore You by God, do not torment me!'"* (Mark 5:6-7). Jesus had no difficulty delivering that man from the plague of demons he suffered.

How could this insane man from another country have known who Jesus was without a formal introduction? Obviously it wasn't the man who was speaking but the demons inside of him. It was not from the exterior that Jesus was recognized. It was what was wrapped up on the inside of His flesh body that they could not take their eyes off. The demons inside that man could clearly see the Spirit of Jesus. There were other times when Jesus would just walk by and demons would manifest in people, shrieking, "*I know who You are--the Holy One of God!*" (Luke 4:34 and Mark 1:24).

People could only see Jesus from the flesh unless the Holy Spirit opened their eyes to who He really was. That is why they only referred to Him as a great prophet or teacher rather than the Christ. But demons could instantly see who He was. They recalled His radiant glory from eons ago, way back before they were excommunicated from the gates of Heaven and fell to the Earth like lightning. They used to worship and adore Him right before His throne. Now they were utterly shocked to see that the Ancient of Days had sneaked onto their turf disguised in an earth-suit. They knew trouble had arrived. They spotted the power and authority He carried before any man could ever detect it.

One time as I was meditating on this scenario, the Holy Spirit came upon me and enlightened me about something. He reminded me that I too am a son of the Most High God. When I understand who I am in this capacity, I can carry myself with the same kind of confidence and authority as Jesus. This is not to make myself equal to Him. He is God and I am not. But we are both sons of God and joint heirs. We are one.

Creatures of the spirit realm see us for who we really are. They know we are of the divine nature. They can see clearly who are God's kids and who are not. They can also see clearly who knows they are a son or daughter of the Most High God and who does not. Think about Paul and the seven sons of Sceva in Acts 19. They tried to cast demons out of people "in the name of the Jesus whom Paul preaches." They didn't get the same results as Paul. Rather than accomplishing a deliverance, they actually got overpowered and beaten up by the demoniac. They ran home stripped naked. All because they tried to experience the benefits of Christ vicariously through Paul.

It is the one who knows who he is and lives like it that gets the most press from both angels and demons. We make the devil shudder when we become aware of our true nature. When the devil and his demons can measure no gap between the truth of who God says we are and our understanding of it, they know they stand no chance in our presence.

It should never be our top priority to have a famous name amongst the demons. A more important goal should be that we know God intimately and know ourselves the way we are known by God. The rest is just the natural by-product. It is not often enough that a demon shouts to a Christian, "I know who you are, a son of the Most High God!" But I believe this will happen more and more as people understand their true identity as God's children.

We need to grow in the revelation of who we are in God. In doing so, it will further be revealed to the world around us. *"For the anxious longing of the creation waits eagerly for the revealing of the sons of God"* (Romans 8:19). Creation needs us to be revealed in fullness as the sons and daughters of the Most High God. This is our present reality. The more we become aware of this truth through the revelation of our status as sons and daughters of God, the more we will begin manifesting this reality until it is known by creation around us. Perhaps when we reach the fullness of this knowledge, we will see the same results Jesus did with the crazy man in the Gerasene graveyard.

A Hysterical Miracle

I used to serve as a prayer servant for a ministry at Bethel Church called Healing Rooms. Every week, the entire Healing Rooms ministry team is amazed at God's miracles of various kinds and we get to hear many reports. They even see the same results go worldwide through Skype on the Internet.

One Saturday morning, after a couple of hours of struggling with the feeling that I was not connecting well with the Spirit, the Lord spoke into my heart regarding the way He wanted me to approach ministry. He told me to take the pressure of performance off of myself and simply love on people with the love of Jesus. What a novel concept! So I shifted my focus from striving for results to simply tapping into the compassion of God's heart.

Later that morning, my prayer partner and I approached a man and asked him what he needed prayer for. He said, "I am just trying to be open to whatever God wants to do with me right now. I don't know if He just wants to love on me, or heal my neck, or shoulder, or knees, or elbows. It doesn't matter. I just want to be open to whatever He chooses to do to me." His name was Grant. We appreciated his humility; but my partner replied, "Well, how about if God just goes ahead and does it all for you?" He was taken off guard and said, "I guess I never thought of that!" So we laid hands on him and invited the presence of God to fall on him. We started ministering the love of Jesus.

Grant got blessed by God's radical touch and began crying out, "Thank You, God! You've been revealing to me this week that I am Your son and You are my Father. Thank You!" I felt impressed to declare over him, "You aren't only God's son. You are His beloved son, in whom He is well pleased!"

He began to cry tears of joy mixed with laughter. He lifted his hands and face up to Heaven to worship God for this revelation. As he was expressing his thanksgiving and love to God, I asked him to check out his neck. He started moving it around. Then he moved it around some more, in every direction. His eyes bulged out and his jaw dropped as he looked at us in awe. He said, "The pain is gone!" He explained that he had received a football injury 19 years ago that left his neck in chronic pain ever since. He was amazed at what just happened.

Then we had him check his shoulder. He lifted his arm up and began to swing it around. Again, he was in awe. His shoulder got damaged over 20 years ago from a motorcycle accident and has been limited in movement and comfort ever since. Now, the pain was gone and full range of motion was restored. This happened before we ever got the chance to even pray for his healing.

He began to jump and shout, "Hallelujah! Hallelujah!" If anyone in the room had never seen a true charismatic before, this was the last day they could say so. It was the most heartfelt shouts of praise I had seen in a long time, and it got the attention of the entire room. The leaders who were orchestrating the flow of the ministry were compelled to bring a microphone to let him share the testimony of his miracle. With everyone expecting him to tell of a divine healing, he instead began his testimony with what mattered most to him. "All week long God has been telling me that I am His son. And now I have seen that He is my Father, and He loves me so much that He wants to give me everything I need. I am His son! He is my good Daddy!"

The atmosphere of the whole room shifted instantly as he shouted his praise and the revelation he had just received. The leader felt there was a special grace on this man's testimony, so he asked if there was anyone in the room who was moved in their hearts with a longing to receive the revelation of their sonship. Many people raised their hands. So he had Grant release a declaration over the room for this revelation of God's Father-heart. It was so powerful! And then Grant grabbed the microphone again, saying, "Oh yeah, and God healed my neck and shoulder completely, and now I have full range of motion with no pain!" Everyone joined in his praise.

Following this, my prayer partner and I went to pray for him one more time for some remaining pains he had in his body from his past ailments and injuries. He said, "You mean God wants to give it all to me?" "Yes," we answered.

We then got to see his elbows and wrists get healed of their chronic pains as well. Praise God! All of these miracles were the result of this man getting the *rhema* understanding that he truly is a beloved son of the Most High God.

We all must win in the battle over our identities. Just as Jesus believed at face value the word God spoke over Him as His Son, and He didn't need proof to aid His faith, we must do the same. We are children of the Most High God. He is absolutely in love with you, and there is nothing you can do to change that. You cannot get Him to love you any more than He already does. And you cannot do anything to get Him to love you any less. His love is infinite and unshakeable. We would do ourselves the greatest favor of our lives to meditate upon this and receive this truth to the degree that we can say, "I am a child of the Most High God, His dearly beloved, in whom He is well-pleased."

6

The Royal Priesthood
– as Priests

What do you get when you place a priest on a throne? A pring? A kiest? A pastor who let his position get to his head? Or how about a pope? Maybe so. But the A+ answer is: *me*... ahem... and *you*, of course.

You and I aren't just simply sons and daughters of God. Jesus Christ is the King of Kings and Lord of Lords. He is King from the lineage of David (Luke 1:32). He is also High Priest in the order of Melchezedek (Hebrews 6:20). In Exodus 19:6, our eternal King and the great High Priest said to His people, "*You shall be to Me a kingdom of priests and a holy nation.*" We are citizens of the Kingdom of God, and He has declared us to be His priests. But we aren't only a kingdom made up of priests. We are *kings* and *priests*.

Holy Priesthood

What an honor for God to call us His priests! This was one of the highest privileges for the Israelites. The tribe of Levi was the only one of 12 tribes that could have priests chosen by God. It was they who were anointed and approved to stand in the house of God and minister in His holy presence daily. They were the ones who had direct access to His Holiness.

But there was only one high priest at any given time. He had privileges that were offered to no one else. He was the one God selected to enter into the Holy of Holies to minister before His very throne, the mercy seat. And this was only one special visit per year. When that day came, the high priest stood awestruck in the midst of the thick, shekinah glory—the weighty, resting, holy presence—of Yahweh. He had a face-to-face encounter with God as the room filled with the smoke cloud of His presence. His ministry was to please God, appease God, and bring an annual atonement to cover the sins of Israel.

Amazingly, under the New Covenant, God has made us to be His priests. It is not based on a Levitical heritage, but on the fact that we are *in Christ*, who is High Priest after the order of Melchezedek. (Melchezedek was a high priest of God who ministered to Abraham three generations before Levi was ever born. According to Hebrews, he had no beginning and no ending. See Hebrews chapter 7.) For us, Jesus has opened the way to the true, greater Holy of Holies in the heavenly places; and we can enter in continually to minister before the mercy seat, the throne of God, freely.

Since the accomplishment of Christ on the cross, we do not have to appease God because Jesus brought the full atonement for the world once and for all. Our priesthood is different in that it is a right to friendship with God. We can worship and adore His Majesty, the Creator of the Universe, close in proximity to His heart.

It is from this position that we are able to move God on our own behalf and that of others. Priesthood is an intercessory right we have; we are given favor to prompt God to release the benefits of His Kingdom into the Earth. Thankfully, we don't have to beg Him to do this because it is already His will. He chooses to partner with us. He sometimes waits for us to exercise our authority to release change into situations. Smith Wigglesworth once said, "If God is not moving, I move Him." That statement may sound arrogant, but Smith understood his position of authority between Heaven and Earth and his favor with God. If nobody else was moving Him, Smith would.

Our proclamations of His will, through prayers and declarations, release the virtues of Heaven from where we are standing into the places where they are lacking. When our words are one with His, the words that come out of our mouth are living and active and become manifested in power in the arenas that we release them. 1 Peter 4:11 says, *"Whoever speaks is to do so as one who is speaking the utterances of God."*

It is from the place of oneness with Jesus, the abiding in Him and He in us, that we are able to bear the fruits of the Kingdom in this life on the Earth. Bearing fruit is a by-product of being connected to a source of life that is rich. It is an outward expression of an inward abiding, drawing from a source of life that comes from some place other than ourselves.

A peach is simply a delicious, juicy, outward manifestation of the life source (sap) drawn through the branch from the heart of the trunk. The outside reflects the virtue contained within. If a nice, juicy, sweet peach can bring so much joy to a person's life, imagine what Jesus can do.

Jesus taught us in John 15 that this is how we are to live with Him. It is a calling to intimacy and union. When we are completely saturated with His richness through and through, like a fruit branch in the thick of season, all of His abounding resources flow outward. This permeation positions us for a manifestation of the supplies of Heaven.

Jesus is teaching us that our priestly prayers go beyond the spiritual sounding petitions of pious humility. For people in the level of intimacy, rest, and fruition that John 15 refers to, our Father is glad to go above and beyond and give the desires of their hearts.

You did not choose Me but I chose you, and appointed you that you would go and bear fruit, and that your fruit would remain, so that whatever you ask of the Father in My name He may give to you (John 15:16).

This is the type of priesthood God has established in His Kingdom. It is not a priesthood of pleading and begging a God who might say "yes" or "no" based on our prayer performance. "Well done, My good and faithful prayer servant. That was a well-polished prayer, uttered with profound, theological jargon. I was particularly impressed with the sweat, tears, and broken blood vessels in your purple forehead, not to mention how proud I am of your bruised and scuffed knees. You have convinced Me that you deserve a lucky break. Make sure you praise Me with that same fervor if you wish to see the remainder of your prayer answered."

Rather, it is the type of priesthood that abides in a union with the Lover of our souls and releases His virtues into the world through us as a by-product. I believe He is more apt to say something like, "Well done, good and faithful daughter. I love how you express your heart of adoration and how you take the time to let me unveil Mine. You are such a beautiful manifestation of My love that I can't contain the desire to lavish you with the riches of My unfathomable grace. Here are the desires of your heart, even the ones you didn't feel worthy to mention. I want this for you more than you want it for yourself. And by the way, thank you for not striving to earn favor with Me, as if you didn't already have more than you know."

David understood this part of God's heart. He scribed it well: "*Delight yourself in the Lord; and He will give you the desires of your heart*" (Psalm 37:4). There is great favor for those who favor the heart of the Lord.

Of course this is not a full discourse on what it is to be an intercessor before the throne of God. There are many aspects of it that I cannot go into at this time. I am not trying to say everything we want or need comes to us at our beck and call. And I am also not saying that there aren't times when we need to persist in prayer, which may include sweat, tears, and bruised knees.

The point I am trying to get across is that true and successful intercession begins at the point of recognizing that we are in union with Yahweh, and we don't need to convince God to do what is already His will. As God's priests, we see the resources of Heaven flow through us from an abiding presence that saturates us and manifests outwardly. Abiding in the Vine, we are branches that bear fruit in every season, which is food for those around us; and our leaves are for the healing of the nations (John 15:5, Ezekiel 47:12, Revelation 22:2). They are by-products of our intimacy.

It is a great joy to be one with Him and partner with His decrees which release manifested goodness into the situations around us. It is a huge privilege that He has made us His priests and given us access into His inner courts. There is nothing of equal value to this highest honor—to access the heart of God.

The Royal Priesthood
– as Kings

A few years ago, the Holy Spirit was revealing some very power-ful truths to me through a series of prophetic words and visions. (Prophecy is simply hearing what God is saying in the moment.) One of the most powerful pictures He showed me was a sword stuck in a stone. The Spirit prompted me to grab the golden handle and pull. When I did, it slid right out of the stone as though it was just resting in butter. I understood this picture as a prophetic symbolism of the legendary (and possibly fictional) King Arthur. Let us take a *Reader's Digest* look at him.

Arthur was a young man of about 15 years old. He was son to Sir Ector, a good knight who was known to be true, faithful, and fairly wealthy. He was brother to the recently knighted Sir Key. Arthur was a handsome, strong, and well-trained knight-to-be himself. On New Year's Eve, a famous tournament was being held in London for the great warriors to come and compete in various sports. The three were on their way to these games as Sir Key was on the roster for a sword-fighting competition. However, Key realized he had forgotten his weapon at home. Arthur was sent back to the house to fetch it, only to discover the doors were locked and nobody was home to help. He had to think of a quick remedy. At this time, he remembered where he had seen another sword.

Hurrying along to St. Paul's church, Arthur found a square stone in the midst of the churchyard, with a naked sword stuck in the middle of it. He reached for the sword and pulled it out of the stone to rush it back to his brother before his match began. When he arrived to his father and brother, they suddenly lost all interest in the knight games because they were astonished to find the lad brandishing the "sword of envy." Arthur must not have noticed the golden inscription on the blade, which said, "Whoso pulleth out the sword from this stone is born the rightful King of Britain."

It was not very long before this time that King Uther had died and left the nation with an empty throne. The country folk were all waiting to discover who the new king would be. When the archbishop gathered all of the people to pray for a sign from Heaven on the matter, there suddenly appeared out of nowhere the stone and the sword containing the prophecy. Arthur seems to have been naive of the fact that there had been many knights, soldiers, and men who tried to pull that sword out of the stone in hopes to become the next king, but all to no avail. Not one man could even budge it. But, for some reason, Arthur pulled the sword out of the stone with ease… like a knife in butter.

Many people gathered around Arthur as he stuck the sword back into the stone and removed it multiple times, and others attempted again with no success. It was finally confirmed that he was God's chosen king for Britain. His father and brother knelt before him in homage. Feeling awkward, he requested they arise as it was not right for a father to kneel to his offspring. It was then that they confessed to him that he was not of their flesh and blood, that he was actually adopted by them when just an infant. It was the best-kept secret. With difficulty swallowing this newfound truth, Arthur finally accepted **who he was not**.

He was then knighted and crowned as king. He took oath to be the true king who would deal justly through his entire life. He then took the trophy sword and placed it humbly on the altar in the church.

While many were excited about their new king, others boiled in rage and a great division was born. Some were just too proud to let a beardless boy rule over them. They were not going to have it. There was an uprising against Arthur's instatement to office.

But Merlin, the great mysterious wise man who always seemed to be part of the revealing of God's will for the nation, stepped in. He pronounced to them all that Arthur was no base adventurer, but was actually the biological son of King Uther, who gave him up for adoption in submission to earlier prophecies. This news was yet another horse pill for Arthur to swallow as the unveiling of truth continued. Merlin told them that they were all bound to serve and honor him as king, as the prophecy on the sword so clearly stated. A great war broke out over this; and, of course, Arthur rose up in strength and conquered his new betrayers.

I can only imagine how he must have been affected by the revelation that his heritage was not due to come to him from the man who raised him; but rather it was to come from a man who he never knew personally. His true father was the king of Britain. Can you say, "Upgrade with rapid rewards"? All in a very short time, he was promoted from ordinary, good ol' boy to high king. At first, he simply earned the position of kingship because he passed a performance test. But once he learned who his true father was, he understood that his royalty went beyond his ability to perform. Royalty was built into his DNA. King Arthur, who once held a mediocre plan for his future, lived on to be a mighty warrior who led the nation into greatness for many years to come.

You see, that sword which I pulled out of the stone in the vision represented my kingdom position which I had to embrace and do something with. The sword represents our calling, our authority, and our freedom to advance into our ordained destinies. But on a deeper note, God was revealing to me that although I have an awesome earthly father, my surpassing Father is Lord of Heaven and Earth. We are sons and daughters of the King of Kings and Lord of Lords. This truth makes us **royalty** in the Kingdom of God.

Kings and Queens

God is simply amazing. Just when you think things couldn't get any better, you discover that He is the gift that just keeps on giving. He is much better than the jelly of the month club. We don't only have the right to stand before His throne as priests; as His children, we each sit at the right hand of the Father in Christ Jesus (see Ephesians 2:6).

Our family is a royal one. We are all children of His Majesty, which makes you and me royal princes and princesses, kings and queens. "*To Him who loved us and washed us from our sins in His own blood, and has made us kings and priests to His God and Father, to Him be glory and dominion forever and ever. Amen*" (Revelation 1:5-6 NKJV). We became royal heirs of the Kingdom of God the moment Christ's blood brought us out of the family of darkness and into His family of light.

It is crucial to understand that, as princes and princesses, we have full access to the King's courts. We truly have a seat with Jesus at the right hand of the Father's throne. He has elevated us above all principalities and powers, and our view of them is **downward** from this position. They are under our feet. He has delegated to us all the authority that is in His Name, not merely as a ranking order in the chain of command, but as His children and heirs. We bear His Name because it is a family Name. He has given to us His signet ring; and the golden key to His Kingdom is ours.

Lessons From a Lad

When my cousin, Sam, was a little boy of about five years old, his dad, Uncle Steve, was an associate minister at a church in Fortville, Indiana. They lived in a parsonage on the same property with the church building. As anyone of his status may, Sam thought he ruled the roost. Exhibiting his rights, he basically did anything he darn well pleased.

For example, one Saturday afternoon, he and his sister, Rachel, were playing in their sandbox in the backyard. Looking up, they noticed there were a lot of cars pulling into the church parking lot. People were dressed up and bearing gifts. This was no party they wanted to miss. He didn't have to work hard to convince sissy. Up they stood and off they went.

Once they got into the foyer, they followed the organ music to where the action was. Everybody was already seated, except for an old man escorting a pretty lady in a long white dress down the aisle. Holding hands seemed right as Sam and Rachel brought up the rear of this small parade. They looked like Pig-Pen from the Peanuts cartoons with a dust cloud that would make a camel choke. They were already halfway down the wedding aisle when an old lady snagged them up before they could turn a white dress brown. For a brief moment, they were the attention of the party. (Which is the story of their lives!)

Another time, Sam and his friend sneaked out of Sunday School to go adventuring. They felt free to roam wherever they fancied because, after all, this was his dad's church. They found a room on the second floor with a window they could open. If it was unlocked, it was fair game. So these five-year-olds climbed out onto a 15 to 20 foot high, narrow ledge and were exploring where it could take them.

After the teacher realized they were missing, she went on a frenzied hunt for them. She may have never found them if it weren't for their whooping and hollering. She climbed out and yanked them back through the window to scold them for their bad behavior. She told them that if they ever did anything like this again, she would have to tell their parents. Sam retorted, "My dad don't care. He owns this place!"

Although Sam may not have represented his father's heart and character well in these accounts (and needed some discipline to help solve this problem), I think he may have been on to something. He understood who his father was and inherently believed that his dad's turf was his turf too. We all need to re-learn the faith of a child who knows who his daddy is. It is in the nature of a child to believe that his parents' property and authority are his own; and they will explore the limits of their perimeters. God is the author of that notion. (This may explain why 30-something years later, Sam's explorations have prepared him to become the pastor of his first church plant.)

Our Father has granted us free and open access into the courts of His Holiness and the infinite, eternal realms of His Heavenly Kingdom.

He wants us to explore and see how far-reaching our potential is in Him. He has given us His signet rings with no holds-barred.

> *Because you are sons, God has sent forth the Spirit of His Son into our hearts, crying, 'Abba! Father!' Therefore you are no longer a slave, but a son; and if a son, then an heir through God* (Galatians 4:6-7).

You have not begun to scratch the surface in pushing your limitations in the estate of Heaven. So take advantage of your freedom to explore and make dreams a reality in the fullness of God. You are an heir! And if anyone ever tries to belittle you and make you feel inferior to the God-sized promises you are reaching for, you can tell him, "My Dad don't care. He owns this place!"

Two Forms of Humility

Now, of course, we don't want to become arrogant in our royal disposition. It does no good to develop a pompous, lofty attitude that makes others feel like we are better than them. I've seen people who look so confident in themselves that they make other people feel intimidated. Many times the appearance of such confidence is really just a self-exerted overcompensation of a low self-esteem.

Humility is always key to greater inheritances in the Kingdom. *"Blessed are the meek, for they shall inherit the earth"* (Matthew 5:5 NKJV). For example, King David was one of the most humble, servant-hearted men of his day. Yet he ruled the greatest kingdom in all of history and was the king who made it reach its highest heights. By the time he passed the torch on to his son, Solomon, it was the most powerful empire of the world. Kings and queens came from great distances to visit Solomon and gawk at his riches and glean from the mysterious wisdom that built this kingdom. But it all was constructed on a foundation laid by a humble, worshipping, servant-king.

Just as David was diligent to avoid pride, we must do the same at all costs. He had every opportunity to take matters into his own hands and think he was great because of it. He could have flaunted his position in pride, but rather he loved and served instead. There were a couple of times when he backslid away from meekness; but when he saw the error of his ways, he was quick to repent and get back into his worshiping position. David knew who was really in charge, and he loved it that way. It is humility that gains favor before the Lord and expands our favor with men.

However, there is another expression opposite to pride that is equally harmful—false humility. False humility errs on the other extreme by acting like there is nothing of greatness within one's self, deferring all excellence to God alone. But let's get real. If God is the amazing Creator that we credit Him to be, we would be foolish to say that we have no greatness. That would be demeaning God's work in our lives. We are great because the Creator is excellent in all of His works. After He made us, He saw that we were very good. We would do well to echo from the heart the words of David in Psalm 139:14— *"I will give thanks to You, for I am fearfully and wonderfully made; wonderful are Your works, and my soul knows it very well."*

True humility acknowledges that God's works are excellent, knowing that He has imparted greatness into us. Take a moment and declare this to God: "Thank you, Lord! For I am fearfully and wonderfully made; wonderful are Your works, and my soul knows it very well." Repeat it until your soul knows it very well.

Humble people live life confidently to their fullest potential, giving God all the glory for bestowing to them the capability to do so. If we lack in this, then we may never reach our full destinies—all for the sake of trying to remain "humble." However, one true definition for meekness is "strength restrained." This means we must know and utilize our strength to its fullest capacity as a service to the King and His Kingdom rather than for selfish gains.

Kings Recognizing the King

The fourth chapter of Revelation gives an amazing picture of what true humility looks like. Twenty-four of the most prestigious, royal people in Heaven are privileged with their own enthronement, surrounding the

Great Throne of His Majesty. An emerald rainbow envelops them as they fix their gaze in awe on His radiant glory that glows in colors like jasper and sardius. (These are deep, fiery, and reddish colors.) At irregular intervals, they have to squint as lightnings flash out and peels of thunder roar. Between their thrones and His are seven living lamps of fire and four Seraphim ministering to the Lord. What must that look like?

The twenty-four elders fall down before Him who sits on the throne and worship Him who lives forever and ever, and cast their crowns before the throne, saying: 'You are worthy, O Lord, to receive glory and honor and power; for You created all things, and by Your will they exist and were created' (Revelation 4:10-11 NKJV).

These men are crowned kings, but they have esteemed their eternal King as far superior. They know who they are and what they have but surrender it wholly to God in worship. This act doesn't change who they are, it just keeps things in the right perspective. We too have been crowned by God and have the opportunity to cast our crowns back to His feet in worship.

I love to picture that scene in light of one of the most exhilarating, adrenaline-pumping scenes in the whole Bible. There will come a time when our King will rise up as a great Warrior dressed for a final battle that will break no sweat on His brow. He will be followed by an immeasurable sea of heavenly hosts ready to charge at His command.

Now I saw heaven opened, and behold, a white horse. And He who sat on him was called Faithful and True, and in righteousness He judges and makes war. His eyes were like a flame of fire, and on His head were many crowns. He had a name written that no one knew except Himself (Revelation 19:11-12 NKJV).

There is so much to wonder about in this epic scene. But the part that really takes my attention is the fact that He has many crowns on His head. Why would He be wearing multiple crowns?

I've been to many rock concerts where the fans were so desperate for their favorite musician's attention. There were a few times when I saw a band member meet an admirer prior to the show, and they gave the musician their favorite hat as a token of honor. When the band member wore that hat on the stage while jamming in front of a crowd of hundreds or thousands, that fan was so thrilled to be honored by his hero's tribute to him.

In a similar way, I believe Jesus is doing the same thing to us. Why does He wear multiple crowns? Perhaps it is because when His worshipers throw their crowns at His feet, He picks them up one at a time and puts them on His head in remembrance and honor of each of His beloveds.

I can see Jesus on the frontline before His innumerous army wearing your crown on His head proudly as He looks over at you with a wink. We truly are royalty, kings giving all honor to our eternal King. He always has us on His mind with great delight. He knows who we are, and that makes it all the more special for Him to wear our crowns. He is called the King *of Kings* for a reason.

Knowing Our Position

Revelation chapter 5 explains how the 24 elders and the four living creatures fell down before Jesus in worship. They were each holding a harp and a golden bowl of incense. They sang a new song that says, "*You are worthy to take the scroll, and to open its seals; For You were slain, and have redeemed us to God by Your blood out of every tribe and tongue and people and nation, and have made us kings and priests to our God; and we shall reign on the earth*" (Revelation 5:9-10 NKJV).

Because we have been redeemed (purchased and reunited) to God by His blood on the cross, we are all destined to reign in God's Kingdom, even here on Earth. We are kings and priests to God.

We must understand who we are. Without this revelation, it is impossible to truly reign. Until you know your position, you will not know your authority or how to use it.

Paul had a strong understanding of his authority and royal sonship. As a good father, he focused on training his disciples in the ways of royalty and sonship to God. At times, he would get frustrated with their lack of maturity after years of training them. For example, speaking sarcastically to the Corinthians as he was trying to bring a gentle correction to them, he said, "*You are already filled, you have already become rich, you have become kings without us...*" (1 Corinthians 4:8). Doing kingdom independently is a paradox. Paul was basically telling them that they had developed their own ideas of what royalty looked like, but those ideas were not in accordance to true kingdom values. It was a somewhat right concept from a very wrong heart motive.

However, with maturity in the revelation of their true nature and its manifestation in their daily lives, they could grow into a true expression of royalty. This is the goal Paul had for them, as he continues, "*... and indeed, I wish that you had become kings so that we also might reign with you.*" Paul is telling us that we are sons and daughters of the eternal King, but it is through the knowledge of and the proper response to who we are that brings us into such a reality. We all can become kings. Reigning is the result.

We were born to reign in royalty. It is our inheritance. However, it is up to us to believe it and live like it, or we will continue on in ignorance just like the Corinthian Christians in their pre-majestic state. We must take our beliefs to a higher level of who we are in Christ as we pursue the revelation of Jesus and the graces that He is extending to us, including the grace of royalty. In the next chapter, we will discuss how He has given us the freedom and the authority to reign in dominion on this Earth, beginning at the place that needs it most.

(If you are interested in learning more about your position of royalty in the Kingdom of God, I recommend you read *Supernatural Ways of Royalty* by Kris Vallotton.)

Dominion is a Birthright

As we read in the previous chapter, Revelation 5:10 says, "(You) *have made us kings and priests to our God; and we shall reign on the earth*" (NKJV). Now that we have established who we are, it is time we take a look at what we should do with this. Does this verse mean Christians are going to rule and reign on this Earth? Does it mean that we are going to dominate and overpower the whole world?

The answer to these questions is yes. However, it does not mean the way that it sounds in this world full of nations, governments, military forces and political movements. A few examples of some dominators that we are familiar with in history are: Julius Caesar, Genghis Khan, the Spanish royalty, the British Imperialists, the American government at times, Hitler, and…Walmart. Each had different methods, motives, styles, and degrees of rulership; but the common goal of each was expansion and dominion.

Back in Jesus' day, this was how the Jews interpreted what the Messiah, the soon-coming King, would be for them. They were sick and tired of living under the Roman Emperor's thumb and were ready for their Deliverer to come and restore the Kingdom of Israel back to the status of King David. Unfortunately, their interpretations of the Messiah were far from God's, and many missed Him. They were greatly disappointed because they were watching the highways for a Messiah who had entered in through the alleys.

Jesus didn't come to establish an earthly kingdom that functions in the way the people of that time were familiar with. He did not

53

come to set them free from the rule of the Roman Empire. He was coming to establish a heavenly kingdom, right here on the Earth. He came to set them free from the rule of a much greater oppressor, the one who influences and rules over the evil men who oppress people— satan and his cohorts. This oppressor can work through more avenues than just military leaders and rulers; he also works through the simple lies individual people believe as they remain enslaved to his lordship.

Jesus brought the Kingdom of Heaven near and established it right in the midst of this Earth, regardless of the kingdoms in power at the time. He had no concern for what the rulers of those kingdoms would think of His work. His Kingdom manifested in small form, fully equipped with a self-contained power to expand in all directions until every place would be filled with it. It cannot be stopped or hindered.

It is like leaven (yeast) spreading through an entire lump of dough. Jesus said, "*The kingdom of heaven is like leaven, which a woman took and hid in three pecks of flour until it was all leavened*" (Matthew 13:33). It starts small, but is a dominating force that imparts and multiplies its DNA into its entire surroundings. Once the Heaven leaven touches the Earth, it is an unstoppable force that spreads until it reaches full saturation.

Jesus is serious about His expansion project. Because it is a kingdom that is the merging of Heaven and Earth, He needs creatures that make their habitation in both realms to co-labor with His works. You and I have a dual-citizenship. We live *in* Heaven *on* Earth.

A lot of people believe that the "reigning-upon-Earth" factor is something reserved for a futuristic millennial reign of Jesus Christ on this Earth. Perhaps that will be true in a way far superior to what we can imagine. However, that does not take away from the fact that it is His full intention for us right now as well. Bill Johnson says, "It is irresponsible to put off something into the future that I could be doing today."

Why do we always read the "we shall" verses as futuristic? When it says, "*we shall reign on the earth*," does it have to just mean later? If that is how we are supposed to read it, I suddenly feel a fresh wave of liberty when I read verses that say things like, "*You shall not steal*" (Exodus 20:15). If "you shall" is a future tense verb, perhaps I can steal until the millennial reign. Of course this idea is absurd. But in the same way, why is it not absurd to assume that all the New Covenant promises which state the inheritances *we shall* have are for the future? Often the word *shall* does by definition refer to future use; but it also can be defined as a present directive of obligation. We need to read carefully when we come upon these phrases to see if they clearly specify a futuristic fulfillment or not. If they do not, I believe they are fair game now *and* later.

> *For if by the transgression of the one, death reigned through the one, much more those who receive the abundance of grace and of the gift of righteousness will* **reign in life** *through the One, Jesus Christ* (Romans 5:17).

God is not waiting until the end of days to begin building towards eternity. What God sets in motion stays in motion until it has accomplished its work in full (see Isaiah 55:11). The ground-breaking ceremony for His restoration and expansion project began on Good Friday a couple of millennia ago. And progress won't stop until His Kingdom has been established in this entire Earth and it is under the complete Lordship of Jesus Christ. This will get accomplished through people like you and me.

We are His ambassadors on this Earth (see 2 Corinthians 5:20), and He has placed us here with His authority to build and expand. When He taught us to pray, "*Your kingdom come, Your will be done, on earth as it is in Heaven*" (Matthew 6:10), this was regarding our kingly role to release His Kingdom on the Earth—to release the capacity of what His will is in Heaven to be mirrored on the Earth.

Redemption

Many times before you begin a restoration project, you have to begin with some demolition. This was where Jesus began. "*For this purpose*

55

the Son of God was manifested, that He might destroy the works of the devil" (1 John 3:8 NKJV). Jesus has already disarmed the god of this world and completely stripped his power from him. He has plundered satan's kingdom and is still reaping the benefits. "*Therefore, since the children share in flesh and blood, He Himself likewise also partook of the same, that through death He might render powerless him who had the power of death, that is, the devil, and might free those who through fear of death were subject to slavery all their lives*" (Hebrews 2:14-15).

Back when Adam and Eve chose to detach from God so they could pursue their own methods of self-fulfillment, they actually were submitting themselves under the lordship of satan's rule. It's always one or the other when it comes to masters. God had intended for them to create the human race under the perfection and wholeness of His glorious Kingdom. Unfortunately, they became subjected to a dark, deathly kingdom of bondage; and it was in that world where they bred the human race. It was under this transfer of allegiance that satan became the "god of this world" where he gained the power to blind people from the light of the gospel of the glory of Christ (see 2 Corinthians 4:4).

Thankfully, the completed work on the cross of Christ disarmed and annihilated the powers of satan once and for all and brought complete redemption to mankind. The chains of our bondage to his darkness have been broken. The locks have been busted and the prison doors have swung open. The strong man has fallen and is crushed under the feet of our Eternal King. Jesus rescued us and set us thoroughly free, and we are free indeed. Anyone who still remains stuck in a prison is in a cage with a door wide open, surrounded by broken chain links all over the floor. All are free to come out and breathe the fresh air under the bright blue skies of Heaven. God is calling His children home.

We have been made free to live in the Kingdom of Light. We are free to enjoy life, to be happy, and to live full of joy and peace. It is OK to laugh and play. We are free to have healthy relationships and to be strong in spirit. We are free to stand before our Lord and Savior and our God and Father without the feeling of guilt and shame. We are free to be full of the Holy Spirit and to overflow with the abundance of His presence continually. We are free to be powerful. We are powerful. He is powerful in us.

Our redemption not only has given us liberty and brought us back into right standing with God; it has completely restored our original state—perfection and blamelessness in His sight. (We will talk about that more in the next chapter.) Adam and Eve, prior to the fall, were the expression of what God had in mind for the human race. They were in complete intimate fellowship and holy union with the Trinity. They were a full manifestation of God's love in physical form. They were God's dream come true. God granted them open passage rights into the entirety of His garden called Eden and full permission to enjoy all of its privileges.

He didn't base relationship on a list of rules. There obviously was no dress code. He didn't give them a book of law, or even ten commandments to follow. He gave them only one rule (to not eat of the tree of the knowledge of good and evil), and everything else was fair game at their own discretion and desire. God never wanted man to have to prove his loyalty through following guidelines. He simply wanted to walk with man in the cool of the day. He wanted to enjoy watching His boy and girl play, discover, and explore, and love, worship, and adore. This is exactly what God has redeemed His children back to through the cross of Christ. And now you are a manifestation of the love of God! You are His dream come true!

Destiny Restored

Our great redemption went beyond the restoration of our status with God. It has also completely restored our destiny in this Earth. What destiny? To rule and reign. After God created His perfect masterpiece, a son in His own image and a wife for him who was crafted with the meticulous handiwork of His gentle hands, He decreed over them a purpose. "*Then God said, 'Let Us make man in Our image, according to Our likeness; let them have dominion over the fish of the sea, over the birds of the air, and over the cattle, over all the earth and over every creeping thing that creeps on the earth*" (Genesis 1:26 NKJV). It is God's plan for His children to have dominion over all the Earth and everything in it.

In order for Adam and Eve to fulfill their purpose, He decreed upon them a mission. "*Then God blessed them, and God said to them, 'Be fruitful and multiply; fill the earth and subdue it; have dominion over the fish of the sea, over the birds of the air, and over every living thing that moves on the earth*'" (Genesis 1:28 NKJV). God blessed them and commanded fruitfulness and multiplication, to fill the earth and subdue it. The word for *subdue* in Hebrew is *kabash* and means "to conquer, subjugate, violate—bring into bondage, force, keep under, subdue, bring into subjection." The job description for God's children was to conquer the world and take dominion, to fill the Earth with His Kingdom.

God had placed Adam and Eve in the Garden of Eden to cultivate and keep it. In essence, He wanted them to expand His lush garden into all the Earth. In order to do this, they would have to conquer any force that would oppose this movement. God is in the business of total domination, and He intends to use His kids to establish His rulership. Under His Lordship, His children get to reign with dominion in this Earth.

When Jesus redeemed us with His blood on the cross of Calvary, He reinstated us into our royal offices. And we now have the same commission He gave to Adam and Eve—be fruitful and multiply, fill the Earth and subdue it, and take dominion. Psalm 24:1 says, "*The earth is the Lord's, and all it contains, the world, and those who dwell in it.*" The owner of the property has made us His legal guardians. He is the King of Kings and the Lord of Lords. We are His delegates in this Earth and He is calling on us to reign in this lifetime. It is up to us to implement His Kingdom.

Jesus reinstated this age-old mission to His disciples using His New Covenant language in Matthew 28:19. "*Go therefore and make disciples of all the nations, baptizing them in the name of the Father and the Son and the Holy Spirit.*" He didn't just request that churches would send missionaries to the foreign nations to win converts from each tribe and tongue, although that is a crucial element of His greater plan. He was commanding the Body of Christ to actually make disciples of nations, which means transforming every aspect of each society and culture into the image of Christ. He fully intends for the Kingdom of Heaven to permeate every earthly kingdom. This requires fruit-bearing, multiplying, filling, and subduing.

In the world, dominion often means to take over and oppress. In Heaven, dominion means to occupy and liberate. Jesus is the Prince of Peace, and He rules and reigns in peace. He desires lordship and there is an order to His Kingdom. But He is in the business of setting people free from oppression. Serving Jesus means liberty. Taking dominion means delivering liberty to all who are oppressed. We are called to dominate over the prince of darkness, as well as his demonic delegates and his lies. We are to plunder the treasures, whom God loves, from satan's kingdom.

The Right Way

The spirit of the world has controlled this Earth for too long. The Body of Christ has remained silent for too long. The condition of this world is not God's fault. He has done everything necessary to set the captives free. He has broken the chains and opened the prison doors. It is up to us to march out of our own hindrances to live in the freedom granted us. It is our job to share this reality with people who are still captive to a false reality. The ball is now in our court. It is our job to take dominion.

The influencing forces of society have been led by the wrong kingdom for long enough. God intends to rule and reign in every realm of society, from Hollywood to D.C. to Harvard to Wall Street (and wherever the influencing cities and culture-shifters are of your nation). He has given the Body of Christ the authority and power to rise up and take ground. He is ready to bless His people who will serve with diligence and integrity and promote us in all the Earth, advancing our favor and our voice.

It will never be accomplished through hating and fighting and picketing and rioting. We've seen these methods fail time and again as they bring embarrassment to the rest of the Church. It won't come through competing or trying to leave the so-called "heathens" in our dust. It will be done through Christ's unconditional love and selfless servanthood. It will only be done by being radically blessed and multiplying, by expanding the Garden of Eden, the Paradise of Heaven, into the Earth around us. It will come by releasing Heaven into the places where it is lacking on Earth. We must carry the same attitude Jesus held—"*Just as the Son of Man did not come to be served, but to serve, and to give His life a ransom for many*" (Matthew 20:28).

God wins by love. He wins by revealing the truth that sets people free and releasing the goods of Heaven into the dry and weary world around us. He is lavishly generous with the riches of His glory and will share it with all who will receive. The world needs the Great Liberation—freedom from the oppression of the spirit of the world.

You Have What It Takes

As sons and daughters of the Most High God, royal highnesses, kings and queens, there is only one person in the whole world who is truly able to overpower us—the Most High God. Every other rule and authority and power and dominion in the spirit realm is under our feet, for we are seated in the heavenly realms in Christ (see Ephesians 1:20-22 and 2:6). Perhaps we can call the rulers of darkness "their low-nesses."

You are from God, little children, and have overcome them; because greater is He who is in you than he who is in the world (1 John 4:4).

The God of peace will soon crush satan under your feet. The grace of our Lord Jesus be with you (Romans 16:20).

And He said to them, 'I was watching satan fall from heaven like lightning. Behold, I have given you authority to tread on serpents and scorpions, and over all the power of the enemy, and nothing will injure you' (Luke 10:18-19).

Regardless of the type of opposition we face, we have this promise: *"In all these things we overwhelmingly conquer through Him who loved us"* (Romans 8:37). As we embrace the truth of God's radical love for us and our union with Jesus Christ, we conquer in all things. He is eager to get this same revelation to all people who have areas that need to be conquered in their lives. The world is full of people waiting for us to bring them this liberating truth. And we can start with "the man in the mirror."

The Headwaters of Dominion

Before we can ever take this multiplying, subduing, and dominating into all the Earth, we must start in places that are more practical. Before you can take the Earth, you have to take a nation. Before you can take a nation, you have to take a region. Before you can take a region, you have to take a city. Before you can take a city, you have to take your personal sphere of influence. But before you can ever take your personal sphere of influence, you first must take yourself. As Leonardo Da Vinci said, "You can have no dominion greater or less than that over yourself."

Ground zero for taking dominion starts with me, myself, and I. God expects us to take dominion in all aspects of our very own lives, including our: walks with God, relationships, emotional and mental states, activities, thought lives, health, finances, schedules, etc. He has given us complete authority and freedom to manage and steward ourselves well. In Christ, we have what it takes to thrive in all areas of life. God desires the richness of the blessings of Heaven to permeate all aspects of our lives. The disciplines of stewardship are part of the pruning which produces greater fruit in us (see John 15).

He wants to see us succeed in taking dominion of the things that are right within reach before we ever try to advance to the bigger realms to reign in. Regarding church overseers, Paul said, *"If a man does not know how to manage his own household, how will he take care of the church of God?"* (1 Timothy 3:5). In the same way, we could say of God's kings and queens, "If a man does not know how to manage his own life, how will he reign in the realms of Earth's societies?"

I am not saying God won't open doors of favor and advancement until we have perfected and mastered every part of life. I am simply saying that our ability to reign outwardly will be a direct reflection of our ability to reign inwardly. God is looking for fruit and growth in each area, regardless of what level of maturity it has attained. We are champions in Christ already by nature. We aren't the only ones who will benefit from reigning over our own lives; our personal victories impact multiplied victories for those we will lead. Remember, dominion in God's Kingdom means bringing freedom to captivity, and it is available for every part of our lives that may lack its abundant fruit.

The most important area we must make top priority in taking dominion is in our belief systems. If we aren't experiencing the rich revelation and manifestation of God's unfailing, radical love in our lives, there is probably something out of whack in our beliefs, because it is available to all. We still have some more conquering to do in our own personal belief systems if we aren't living in the full awareness of being: children of the Most High God, partakers of the divine nature, kings and queens, spirits in union with the Holy Trinity. Most of us have at some point been sold a lie that we are underdogs and inferior in the Kingdom of God. We must take dominion over our beliefs!

My mentor, Steve Backlund, frequently talks about a period of his life when God taught him where his spiritual warfare needed to begin. God told him to take his large spiritual machine guns that are pointed at the enemy and turn them inward to get the sights lined up on his own mind. "Ready, aim, FIRE!" He passed on to us a quote from a book by Francis Frangipane called *The Three Battlegrounds* that has changed his life. "Any area of my life that is not filled with glistening hope is where I am believing a lie and is a stronghold of the devil." Steve goes on to explain, "That means that spiritual warfare has much more to do with what I believe than with binding and rebuking."

God has given us hope. It is up to us to take it. Everything He has done for us is enough to give us glistening hope. What more can you ask for than *"Christ in you, the hope of glory"* (Colossians 1:27)? That is an all-encompassing promise.

True spiritual warfare begins with our thought life. We need to bring it under subjection to the truth of Christ, which often defies the way our minds tend to think. Second Corinthians 10:5 says we are *"casting down arguments and every high thing that exalts itself against the knowledge of God, **bringing every thought into captivity to the obedience of Christ**"* (NKJV). Whatever thoughts we have that do not line up with what God says need to be brought into captivity to the obedience of Christ. A great place to begin is to recognize the lie and then declare the truth over it from the Scriptures. Jesus modeled this well in the wilderness in Matthew chapter 4 when He was tempted by the devil.

Because we live in a fallen world that is sending false messages to us constantly, we should all be applying this exercise on a regular basis. It is for the renewing of our minds. *"And do not be conformed to this world, but be transformed by the renewing of your mind, so that you may prove what the will of God is, that which is good and acceptable and perfect"* (Romans 12:2).

God is cleansing out the old ways of thinking and instilling His ways of thinking. He is restoring to us the mind of Christ (see 1 Corinthians 2:16). As our minds line up with His, our lives will outwardly accelerate into the manifestation of His expanding Kingdom. As Steve Backlund says, "Our experiences are catching up to our beliefs."

Exterior Manifested From Within

Please do not go out and try to win a third-world nation before you have personally experienced at least some significant measure of personal breakthrough in what you are trying to give to them. Please do not try to set a region free from a demonic principality if you haven't yet discovered how utterly free you are yourself. We can only give away what we have. But we first must understand what we have before we can effectively give it away.

It happens often that people pursue spiritual battles to fight that are greater than what their spiritual foundations are prepared to withstand and wind up defeated. It is like being so eager to build a house that you don't want to wait for a proper foundation to be laid, so you throw it together upon the sandy beach. However, we all know what happens when the storm comes (see Matthew 7:24-27).

For example, I wouldn't recommend going on a mission trip to a "Burning Man" festival if you are still overcoming weakness to lust. ("Burning Man" is a weeklong party in the desert of Nevada with thousands of free-spirited individuals, many of which like to run around naked.) Perhaps a bar ministry wouldn't be the best option for a recovering alcoholic to pursue in their zeal for Christ. Starting a marriage counseling ministry probably isn't the best plan for a recent divorcee.

On a more practical note, God's ultimate calling on your life is probably far beyond what you are currently prepared to handle. This just means that we all need to go through seasons of growth and/or inner healing in order to develop a foundation that can support the weight of what He plans to build. Shortcutting the process can be detrimental. It is so important to let the Holy Spirit establish freedom and maturity in our hearts and to take dominion in proportion to the stage of the process in which He has us.

If you have already gone in over your head in this way, it's probably a good idea to pull back and have a rest in the Lord. Let the healing begin. Spend time letting the Holy Spirit saturate you with His radical love and the truth of how free you really are in Christ. Get it into your core. Let it saturate every fiber of your being. Let this revelation become the foundation you live from for the rest of your life. Let your ministry overflow from it.

There is nothing you can do for God that is more powerful than this. Your work will prove more effective on the other side of this revelation. Our capacity to minister freedom to other people is directly proportional to how free we are within ourselves.

"You will know the truth, and the truth will make you free" (John 8:32). The truth is that we are completely and utterly set free by the love of Jesus Christ and the victory of the cross. In Christ, there is no longer anything that has the power to bind us…except one thing—believing a lie. This is the devil's only hope, which is why he is the father of lies. He has waged a full-on war with our beliefs. If he can get us to consider his lies, he has us bound. But if we can believe truth, we will live freely. Truth wins every time!

Believing a lie that something or someone, other than yourself and God, is powerful enough to control you can give you the experience of not being free. Believing a lie that some ungodly desire or action is part of your nature or inheritance can give you a false experience which does not match up with the truth that you are a new creation. Believing a lie that circumstances control your ability to live righteously will cause you to not live righteously. But it does not change the truth that Jesus has already broken the chains off you. You can believe the lie that you are still a victim and prisoner and remain stuck in place. But it does not change the truth that Jesus has already busted down the cell door, cleared out a safe passageway outside of the dungeon, and is ready to escort you into the land of the free.

Knowing the truth that we are free will make us free indeed (see John 8:32). We must grow in the revelation of how free we **already are** in Christ. It is a progressive revelation that brings greater levels of freedom in our beliefs and, furthermore, our experiences. We need the Holy Spirit to continue tutoring us into maturity. We must take dominion over our thought lives and belief systems so we can fully understand the totality of our freedom and our radical union with the Holy Trinity. The effectiveness of the power of Christ's accomplishment on the cross to deliver and provide solutions to our problems is not contingent upon favorable circumstances. It is infinitely powerful, eternally present, abundantly available, and will conquer anything that opposes it!

The more our inward dominion gets established, the more our outward dominion will manifest with increasing strength and range. That is just what happens. Blessing and multiplication happen through the revelation of who we are in Christ and who He is in us, expanding His Garden outward in every direction.

In order to take greater dominion in ourselves, we must go further in our revelation and personal beliefs of who we are to God and who He is to us. This will be our topic in the next chapter.

God is Judging You

D id you know that God is looking for nothing less than perfection in His people? He is perfect and anything less than that is not qualified to stand in His presence. His holiness is too pure for things tainted with imperfection. In Exodus 19, God commanded that no one touch His holy mountain except Moses, or they shall die. In 2 Samuel 6, Uzzah attempted to save the Ark of the Presence from falling to the ground when it nearly dropped off of the ox-cart, and the anger of the Lord burned against him and instantly struck him dead for touching the Ark with unqualified hands. God does not allow imperfection near His holiness.

Lucifer was kicked out of Heaven because there is no room for pride. Adam and Eve were excommunicated from the Garden of Eden because sinfully-tainted people should have no access to the Tree of Eternal Life. The examples are many.

These could be very discouraging thoughts for us. Perhaps this is why so few people get to experience the deeper encounters in the inner courts of His holy presence. But it is not because of our inadequacies as much as it is our ignorance of the truth about how God sees things. And as I have said a time or two before, how we view things will determine what we experience. We must learn to examine what He is looking at.

You see, as far as God is concerned, if you have set yourself apart to live as a child of God through the one time, all-encompassing, eternally-enduring sacrifice of Jesus, you have been qualified. *"For by one offering He has **perfected for all time** those who are sanctified"*

(Hebrews 10:14). Jesus has already made us perfect in His sight, and it is for all time. Our perfection is determined by our choice to be set apart (sanctified) unto God through faith.

Don't get me wrong. This doesn't mean that everything we do or think is perfect. We still need to be renewed in our minds daily. But God's view of perfection is different from ours. It has nothing to do with anything we have done or not done. It has everything to do with what Jesus has done for us through His perfect and complete work on the cross and our active faith in this. When your old man became crucified with Christ on the cross (Galatians 2:20), Christ put into you a new perfect spirit, which is the essence of who you are in Him. It is a fusion of your spirit and the Spirit of Christ made one.

We are continually being outwardly transformed more and more into the image of Christ that already exists inwardly; which in essence means we haven't arrived fully yet in manifested form. However, God chooses to look at us in our state of completion—"*Declaring the end from the beginning*," He says, "*My purpose will be established, and I will accomplish all My good pleasure*" (Isaiah 46:10). Paul said, "*I am confident of this very thing, that He who began a good work in you will perfect it until the day of Christ Jesus*" (Philippians 1:6). God sees from the front end a perfected son and daughter, and He is committed to make our external world (thoughts, behaviors, and environments) catch up to our interior world (perfected spirit).

Galatians 3:27 says, "*For all of you who were baptized into Christ have clothed yourselves with Christ*." We are all wrapped up in Jesus Christ, and that is what God sees when He looks at us. Between the fact that He presently sees our perfected end product and Jesus Christ covering us all over, we have been officially qualified to stand before Him with confidence. In spirit, we truly are perfect, and that is where it matters most.

"*For He chose us in Him before the creation of the world to be holy and blameless in His sight*" (Ephesians 1:4 NIV). It is already settled. God has already chosen that those of us who are in Christ would be holy and blameless through Him. This is God's judgment upon us. He judges us as holy; we are without blame. To God, we are perfect, holy, and blameless. It really can't get much better than that!

Entries in God's Journal

A lot of people believe that God is frustrated and ready to bring His wrath upon them if they do something wrong. They feel like they are walking on eggshells, as if they might arouse His uncontrolled anger or deep disappointment in them. I used to try really hard to make sure I was doing my best to keep God happy with me. (I have never liked the thought of letting Him down.) Little did I know how wrong my thinking was. He was already pleased with me because I am His beloved son. He doesn't want us to work *for* love; He wants us to work *from* love.

God is so much better than we give Him credit for. Yes, there is a wrath from God for sin. However, as we previously discussed, He has already taken it out upon Jesus, who bore our sins upon Himself. There will be another day in the future for the Great Judgment. But we have two things in our favor. One, right now is not a time of judgment. The first judgment was 2000 years ago on Calvary, and the next will be in an age yet to come. We are living in the age of grace, which happens to be an eternal virtue.

The second thing we have going for us is that we are exempt from that great judgment of wrath altogether. It is reserved for satan and all who have never abandoned his kingdom in order to enter into God's (see Revelation 20:11-15). So, as children of the Most High God, the wrath of God is not even on our radar. If it is showing up on yours, it is time to scrap that piece of junk and find a new and improved one for your viewing pleasure. My tracking device is homing in on His glory, not His wrath. If you read through the book of Revelation, you will find that the wrath of God has nothing to do with those whose names are written in the Lamb's Book of Life. Our judgment is not one of wrath but of reward for the accomplishments we have done on Earth.

Of all the things that God wants to see in His children, He would never expect anything from us that differs from His ways. Anything God requires from us in character or practice is in accordance with the nature of who He is as a person; and He has bestowed to us His nature. 1 John 4:8 says that God is love. If He is, then we can learn some things about His character in 1 Corinthians 13:4 which says, *"Love is patient, love is kind."* If God is love, then we can equate this to also mean that "God is patient, and God is kind." 1 Corinthians 13:5 says love *"keeps no record of wrongs"* (NIV).

This virtue of love keeping zero records for wrongs begins with God. We all have done (and still at times do) wrong things that offend His heart. Regardless of this fact, as far as He is concerned, we are still holy and blameless before Him. He is not making a list of which of His kids are being naughty or nice; nor does He outsource that job to the North Pole.

Under the Old Covenant we would all be in heaps of trouble. It was a law based on rights and wrongs. It was a system of rules based purely on behaviors, and if you would break one law, God considered all broken. *"For as many as are of the works of the Law are under a curse; for it is written, 'Cursed is everyone who does not abide by all things written in the book of the Law, to perform them'"* (Galatians 3:10). Although it was an order that inspired full effort to obtain perfection, it was an external and self-exerted religion. There was no intimacy involving the heart of God in the law.

Thank God there is a New Covenant! Many years before it was instituted, the Holy Spirit forecasted what this superior one would look like.

> *'But this is the covenant which I will make with the house of Israel after those days,' declares the Lord, 'I will put My law within them and on their heart I will write it; and I will be their God, and they shall be My people. They will not teach again, each man his neighbor and each man his brother, saying, "Know the Lord," **for they will all know Me**, from the least of them to the greatest of them,' declares the Lord, **'for I will forgive their iniquity, and their sin I will remember no more'*** (Jeremiah 31:33-34).

The New Covenant was cut 2000 years ago in the flesh of the Sinless One who bore the sins of the world. Through the shedding of His blood, we now live in freedom according to a law that is based on a heart-to-heart relationship with God. He has forgiven our iniquity, and He does not remember our sins. He would literally have to die again before He would allow Himself to remember our sins because covenants last until "death do us part."

As far as God is concerned, sin is no longer grafted into our nature. When we became one with Christ in His death, burial, and resurrection, our sinful nature died, and we were made alive in purity and wholeness. This is why Paul said, "*Even so consider yourselves to be dead to sin, but alive to God in Christ Jesus*" (Romans 6:11). Peace has been thoroughly made between God and us; it is the theme of His covenant. He has tossed aside the old book that archived all the wrongs we've done. The only book He is reading up on about you and me is the Book of Life, which is a journal of all that Jesus has done and is doing in us.

Shepherd's Encounter

Imagine that you are a shepherd of old going through the daily grind of the dirty and typically boring routines of the job. Every day, you are out in the fields overseeing the sheep with the simple task of keeping them corralled together and watching for predators as they graze the grass. I think it would get pretty mundane. An occasional coyote might actually be a welcomed guest just to spice things up a bit. Entertainment would probably sink to such lows as inventing creative games like hopscotching around sheep pebbles.

This may be why David kept a slingshot and a harp in his manpurse to fool around with. He needed something to occupy his time. He probably got tired of censusing the sheep—a task so tranquilizing it could have knocked him out cold one too many times.

The shepherds outside of Nazareth must have been feeling the same way on the night the Savior was born. It was just another round of the same humdrum monotony. If you would ask them "What's up?" they would probably just sigh, "Ahhh, same sheep, different day." I picture them laying around a campfire, playing tunes while eating rancho beans like the cowboys in *Blazing Saddles*. They had no idea any headline news was breaking, because to them it was just another dull day in Paradise.

That is, until the moment an angel of the Lord suddenly appeared before them with the shekinah glory transfiguring the pitch-dark campsite into a glowing, radiant, ethereal ambiance. This frightened the shepherds probably more than when I used to sneak up behind Grandma while she was watching Frankenstein and yell, "BOO!" into her only functioning ear. She jumped out of her seat with a scream that scared me right back; and we all got drenched in a shower of Diet Coke and popcorn. These shepherds saw what they would have never expected for themselves and were immediately startled.

They were instantly aware of the holy presence of God surrounding them, an experience they only could imagine was reserved for the high priest once a year. They were unworthy of such an encounter and knew the consequences, thus even more reason for fear and trepidation.

But the angel proclaimed, "*Do not be afraid; for behold, I bring you* **good news of great joy** *which will be* **for all the people***; for today in the city of David there has been born for you a Savior, who is Christ the Lord*" (Luke 2:10-11). This angel was informing these lowly men that they need not fear the presence of the Lord anymore. God's terms were changing. Rather than wrath for bringing uncleanness into His presence, He was telling these dirty, unkempt men that they can relax. God was sending good news of great joy for all people, including them. It was time for the chapter of the fear of God's wrath to be closed so the new chapter of God's great joy and acceptance could be introduced.

Why was this shift taking place? Because the Savior of the world, the promised Messiah, was born, and a new era was dawning. Emmanuel was brought into our world. "God is with us!"

Now, mankind would discover that God was in a good mood, desiring great joy for all people. This was His good news.

As if that weren't enough to blow their grids, their eyes then became opened to see even more. All of a sudden, an innumerous host from Heaven surrounded the messenger, filling the air. What had been a dark night sky became like the high-noon sunshine as all of these angels illumined the entire atmosphere around them. Their glowing garments permeated with the radiant residue of glory that protruded from being in the presence of the throne they had just come from. "*Glory to God in the highest, and on earth **peace among men with whom He is pleased**,*" they praised in beautiful harmony (Luke 2:14). They were glorifying God as they proclaimed that **He was at peace with men and actually pleased with them!**

This was quite the shift of revelation for these ranchers. Now they had learned that the Christ was born, bringing great joy, peace, and pleasure from God to all people on the earth. God not only had bestowed peace upon broken hearts, He announced through His angels that He was at peace with mankind within His own heart. When the angels left to return to Heaven, these distressed men were glowing with joy and filled with new purpose. No longer afraid to stand in the presence of God, they went to worship in person the Son of God who was made manifest in flesh.

After a warm visit with the newborn King of Kings, they left glorifying and praising God for all they had seen and heard. These men were probably intimidated by people of higher stature than themselves prior to this night. But after an encounter with Jesus Christ, they became emboldened as the Lord's first evangelists to proclaim His good news.

God is Not Angry

The fact is that God is not angry. He actually is in a very good mood. I laugh at the idea of God constantly shifting back and forth from happiness to anger based on our instabilities. If you think about it, that makes Him seem quite immature and unstable Himself. He is not bi-polar, nor is He one to be easily moved.

I really like what my friend, Kayo Zukowski, once said: "From the time of Adam to the time of The Flood was about 1600 years. That means it took God 1600 years to become grieved in His heart (see

Genesis 6:6). And from the time of The Flood to the Tower of Babel was about 800 years. That means it took God another 800 years to get angry." And that was before the New Covenant was in effect. God is not ticked off at us like people have been duped into believing.

On the contrary, He is so full of joy! Hebrews 1:9 says about Jesus, "*You have loved righteousness and hated lawlessness; therefore God, Your God, has anointed You with the oil of gladness above your companions.*" As my friend, Beatrice Parlbage, recently commentated in her sermon, "Jesus is literally the happiest person in the world!" We shouldn't take this for granted. There was a reason why Jesus was nicknamed the Wine Bibber. It is not because He was a drunkard, but because His fullness of joy is at a level that can offend the average religious person. Imagine the 'Wine Bibber' also being the 'Friend of Sinners.' Was the Holy One really happy when hanging out with people who were full of sins and offenses? Why should His blessed children ever think less of ourselves in His presence?

Whatever God reveals to us about His nature is what He is offering to make manifest into our own lives. For example, let's take a look at Galatians 5:22-23: "*The fruit of the Spirit is love, joy, peace, patience, kindness, goodness, faithfulness, gentleness, self-control; against such things there is no law.*" This isn't merely a list of requirements God is expecting out of us. It is actually the very nature of the Holy Spirit. He is absolutely full of love, joy, peace, patience, kindness, goodness, faithfulness, gentleness, and self-control. They are expressions of who He is. Furthermore, they are a few of the many good things He is giving out freely to anyone who will receive. It is always a free gift, and it comes from simply being filled with the Holy Spirit and letting go of striving by our own strength.

Galatians 5:18 tells us that if we are led by the Holy Spirit, we are not under the law. As a matter of fact, if we live by the Spirit, we furthermore will not carry out the desires of the flesh (see Galatians 5:16). The reason is because God's New Covenant has been written on our hearts and minds through the Holy Spirit, as stated earlier in Jeremiah 31:33. It is no longer about rights and wrongs but about relationship through the Holy Spirit within us. We are no longer living by the sinful nature but by the Holy Spirit. Just as sinful thoughts and actions used to come so naturally, now all the more, the fruits of the Spirit are natural by-products from living in union with Him.

Embracing the truth that His attributes of love, joy, peace, patience, kindness, goodness, faithfulness, gentleness, and self-control are His expressions of acceptance toward us causes them to take root and spring forth life within our own hearts as well. They are supernatural qualities that become natural traits to the children of God. It is no longer about us trying to produce these traits in our lives; it is about us knowing who this God is who loves us dearly. Then the fruits just happen within us from being connected in heart.

It blows my mind to think of all God has done to graft my nature into His and His into mine. Because I am one with Him and He with me, I carry His DNA in my spirit and He has made me prone to righteousness. As the nature of the Holy Spirit lives and flows through me outwardly, my external reality begins to increasingly reflect my internal reality. God has already perfected my spirit man in Christ and has qualified me in full to stand righteously in His presence. I am holy and blameless before Him because I am in Christ. The only record God is keeping on my life is about the fruit He is bearing through me as I am being transformed outwardly into the image of Christ that is already within me. This is your reality just the same.

10

Back to the Creek

There was a season in my life when the Lord was teaching me about His heart towards me regarding my sin and repentance. Sometimes it takes me awhile to learn new lessons, and He has to really work with me. There were three particular encounters I had that I want to be transparent with so I can share about the heart of the Lord. They each came with a quote from the Bible that He dropped into my heart as *rhema*.

"Who Told You that You're in Sin?"

Back when I was in my early twenties, I was passionately in love with Jesus and gave everything I had to Him. He was so good to me and was bringing me into fresh revelation of who He was. I had just spent a year away from home in Bible college getting radically transformed in my faith and stepping into more and more personal encounters with Him. I can remember many instances when Jesus would fill my bedroom with His glory and would come and speak the mysteries of His heart to me. They were thrilling times that, thankfully, still happen today.

Even in the midst of these great seasons of glorious intimacy, I still had my personal battles. I was a victorious mighty man of valor, conquering my archenemy whenever he brought an onslaught at me…most of the time. In those days, I tried my best to keep my armor on and my binoculars up to continually watch for the enemy before he'd come striking. However, this enemy was smart and patient to wait until the moments he found me relaxing my vigilance. Then he would send "covert ops" agents from his fort to infiltrate my territory by stealth and take me down when I least expected it.

They didn't ambush me all at once. They stayed hidden and lured me into a trap. Sometimes they would begin by tossing into my memory bank a quick snapshot image of an obscene picture I had seen before. Then, after a few moments of rest from the image, as to not give away their position, they would toss another scene in for a moment. Their strategy was to make me believe these thoughts were actually my own.

When I was in an unguarded, vulnerable frame of mind, these enticements would grow to a strength that eventually would override and weaken my willpower. Their hypnotizing mental flashes worked like a poison gas, drugging me until my mental disposition shifted into submission. Finally, they would throw in an indulgence grenade, and I would cave in under pressure. Jumping from behind his little fortress, Major Lust would run over and pin me to the ground in a full nelson to handcuff me and keep me in holding until his superior arrived.

As most everyone has experienced, after the short-lived pleasure came to its end, Colonel Shame would promptly show up to the scene to enforce martial law. I would be branded with a big "S" on my forehead to label me as "Sinner." And I was tried, convicted, and sentenced to condemnation.

I was smart enough to know that the enticement to lust came from the demonic realm. The Bible is clear about who is trying to steal, kill, and destroy us. I knew that *"our struggle is not against flesh and blood, but against the rulers, against the powers, against the world forces of this darkness, against the spiritual forces of wickedness in the heavenly places"* (Ephesians 6:12). That was easy to accept. What I did not understand was that the guilt and shame I carried was also from the same forces.

I knew I had done wrong and my actions and thoughts had grieved God. There is no peace in the thought of grieving Him. Carrying guilt and shame was the least I could do to bear the weight of the sin I had committed. Oh, I was so deeply sorry for what I had done. Godly sorrow had led me to ardent repentance. I asked Jesus to forgive me of my sins and cleanse me from them. I pleaded with Him to break the sinfulness off of me and take it away. I mourned over my actions with great lamentations.

No matter how hard I would try to repent, I couldn't feel any better. I'm not really sure I was yet ready to feel better though. I needed to be punished for what I had done, and grief was doing a good job. It's not that I wanted to feel this way. My true desire was to make God happy with me so we could be reunited. I believed that if I could reach a certain level of despair over my sin, I could appease His heart, convincing Him to draw me back into intimacy again.

I lived at Mom and Dad's house out in the countryside at this time. There was a field behind their house that I would regularly hike through to get to a wooded stream. It was one of my favorite prayer spots. In my agony of repentance, I actually built an altar out of stones I had gathered from the creek. It was a noble gesture.

After hours of laborious prayer and begging, the Lord showed up and spoke to my aching heart in the still, small voice that I hadn't yet taken time to listen for. What He said was not what I would have expected to hear. That one sentence instantly halted my penance in its tracks.

He said, "Who told you that you are in sin?" I immediately knew that what He asked was of the same nature as when He asked Adam and Eve, "*Who told you that you were naked?*" (Genesis 3:11). Adam and Eve's nakedness had never been an issue to God; it was how He created them to be. He knows what is beautiful, no doubt. The nature of their nakedness before the fall was morally pure and absent of lust. God loved it and gave it to them as a gift. They had no reason to be ashamed of it. But the spirit of condemnation had come upon them after they rebelled against God's command to not eat of the tree of the knowledge of good and evil.

Everything God had created He called good, including them and their nakedness. He had already given them the knowledge of all that is good the moment He created them in His image. He actually intended to keep them eternally and altogether ignorant of anything evil for their safety and purity. In that condition, they could have always lived a life that was focused exclusively upon God and everything good and never even taste of badness. He never wanted anything more.

Because they chose to expand their knowledge beyond the realm of God's goodness into the realm of evil, their eyes were opened to things they would soon regret. They had lifted the lid off of Pandora's box and hell broke loose. When God asked who told them they were naked, He knew they had drunk from the cup of delusion that only the deceiver could pour. God did not judge them as naked; and He never wanted them to judge themselves either. To Him, they were good in their nakedness. To Him, they were covered in His goodness. But they saw something in themselves that He could not see. Are those the kind of glasses we want to look through? The kind that shows things God doesn't even see? Condemnation gave them a distorted self-image.

I knew what God was saying when He asked, "Who told you that you are in sin?" He was revealing to me that the moment I first asked Him to forgive my sin, it was forgiven and forgotten. 1 John 1:9 says, "If we confess our sins, He is faithful and righteous to forgive us our sins and to cleanse us from all unrighteousness." I was begging God to forgive me and cleanse me of something that was non-existent. He showed me that all the toil, labor, and tears that I had put into my penance were actually ignorantly done in vain. All of those hours and days that had gone by while bearing the weight of my sin on my own shoulders turned out to be wasted time. Jesus had already taken the sin and born it on the cross for me.

The moment I asked for forgiveness, I was in union with what He had already taken care of. All of this time, He was standing before me just waiting for me to look up from His feet into His face so I could listen to His heart. I was slowly learning by the ounce that my grief does not appease God's anger for my sins, but it had already been satisfied through Jesus on the cross. I just needed to believe.

Am I saying God justified my behavior? Absolutely not. All sin is completely and utterly detestable to God. There is no excuse for sin.

But God did not justify my sins. He justified me, separate from my sins.

As soon as I heard God's loving words, I took a deep breath, and peace flooded my soul. The guilt and shame were lifted off my neck, and I was instantly restored into the deep, intimate love of Jesus. His presence surrounded me and brought me into a beautiful encounter. I was back to my normal, confident self again. I no longer had to avoid people who needed me to minister the love of God to them. I could live on and feel secure. My dignity had been restored. Who told me that I was still in sin? Well, obviously it was not God. And if God didn't say it, I shouldn't believe it.

"Don't Call Unclean What I Have Called Clean"

Some time after this incident, I actually came upon another. The vicious cycle revolved back around, and again I got the smackdown. Same old story, different day. It was the same routine of letting my guard down after lots of warfare and battle. Sometimes even a soldier needs a break, right? But I was learning that when you take a break spiritually, you get spiritually broken. When I took a rest from being spiritually-minded, the devil broke my neck and paralyzed me with guilt and shame all over again. Once more, I was back to the creek.

In my toil and gut-wrenching repentance over that mound of rocks, I had forgotten the last session God taught. I thought I was not worthy of His goodness until I had born the full weight of my sin. Even though He showed me how easy it was to get clean last time, it surely could not be the same this time because of how soon it had been since then. There was not enough time spaced in-between my failures for easy repentance. In my eyes, this sin was stacked upon the prior, making it twice as tall.

After hours and days of pleading with God for mercy, I finally exhausted myself and came to a lull. In my quieted fatigue, I felt Him gently tapping my shoulder. He said to me, "Do not call unclean what I have called clean." When I heard this, it shook me up. He was defending me from myself. I was being rebuked by Jesus for calling myself unclean.

He revealed to me the same lesson as before: that at the very moment when I sincerely asked Him for forgiveness, I was thoroughly and utterly forgiven. Any request of forgiveness beyond this was in vain, for it revealed unbelief that God had actually done what He had promised. My sins previously committed were no longer my sins. They were non-existent. My heart had been deeply rinsed clean in the blood of Jesus, and all God could see in there was utmost purity. He declared that I was clean.

This statement was the same one God had spoken to Peter in Acts 10. He put Peter into a trance and gave him a vision. Peter saw the sky open up and a giant tablecloth floating down with non-kosher animals on it, such as pork, rattlesnakes, and lobsters, which were forbidden for the Jews to eat. God spoke and said, "*Get up, Peter, kill and eat!*" Peter in his religious zeal replied, "Not a chance, Lord! You know I have never eaten anything unholy and unclean" (my paraphrase). God answered, "*Do not call anything impure that God has made clean*" (Acts 10:15, NIV).

It was God who had given the commandments in the Old Covenant to consider such animals unclean and never to eat them. At one time, He had considered them unclean. But now that He had established a New Covenant, He was revealing that He no longer considered them as such. If He called something clean, He would expect us to call it clean as well. Anything less would be utter rebellion.

This vision was to prepare Peter and the apostles to accept the Gentiles as clean, which were previously considered unclean according to the old order God had established. Under the new order, all old things have passed away and all things have become new (see 2 Corinthians 5:17).

If God calls something clean that we consider unclean, it is time for a paradigm shift.

I was calling myself unclean because I was judging myself for a sinful action that I had committed prior to the cleansing of Jesus' blood. Once I asked for forgiveness, the sin was sent to the cross and dematerialized into nothingness by the blood of Jesus. In continuing to agonize over something nonexistent, I was still calling myself unclean and partnering with a vain imagination. God had already declared me clean, and He was calling on me to change my confession. As soon as I understood what He was saying, I accepted my cleanness and realized I was worthy to stand tall in His presence again. There is no shame where there is a clean heart.

"You Are Clean Because of the Words I Have Spoken to You"

I've heard it said that repetition is the mother of learning. I have to say, after these two encounters with God revealing His instant mercy, I was beginning to latch on and take it in. When the next time rolled around that I stumbled into sin, which grieved my heart as I knew it did His, I repented with caution. I felt horrible for what I had done, but I did not want to bring additional grief to God by my unbelief in His mercy. I knew now that when I asked Him to forgive me, it would surely be done.

Still, I could not shake the feeling of shame. I tried to but couldn't. I knew He was faithful in His promises, but I still carried that deep feeling of being unclean. I had learned my lesson about stewing in guilt. So I looked to the Lord to ask for help as I trusted He would not leave me hanging out to dry. I was not disappointed as I found that this was the exact opposite of what He was about to do.

Before I could even get a word of repentance out of my mouth, He beat me to the punch (not literally) and did not give me the chance to get a word in edgewise. He said, "You are already clean because of the word which I have spoken to you." Now, it is very important to confess sin and ask for forgiveness once sin has been committed. God needs a heart that chooses Him over sin. But the Lord knows the heart before the mouth even speaks, and His response is faster than the electrical pulses that shoot through the nerves from the brain to the tongue. I couldn't even blurb a syllable, and He had forgiven me; I was already clean.

His words were a direct quote from John 15:3. In that passage, Jesus explains that He is the Vine and we are His branches, if we abide in Him and He in us. He explains that His Father is the Vinedresser who takes away branches that bear no fruit and prunes the ones that do. It says "*every branch that bears fruit, He prunes it so that it may bear more fruit*" (John 15:2).

The Greek word for "prunes" is *kathairo*, which means "to prune or purge" but also means "to cleanse." It comes from the root word *katharos*, which means "clean, clear, and pure." *Katharos* is the word Jesus used in John 15:3 when He said, "*You are already clean* (Greek: katharos) *because of the word which I have spoken to you.*" The word of Jesus actually cleanses the one who has ears to hear. It is also the same word He used in Matthew 5:8 when He says, "*Blessed are the pure* (Greek: katharos) *in heart, for they shall see God.*" Jesus' spoken word does not cleanse us just to make us clean; it brings us into a place where we are actually able to see God.

There is so much power in the words of Christ. When He speaks, lives are radically changed in the blink of an eye. When He speaks, it is a natural by-product that we are cleansed. Ephesians 5:25-27 says, "*Christ also loved the church and gave Himself up for her, so that He might sanctify her, having **cleansed** her by the washing of water with **the word**, that He might present to Himself the church in all her glory, **having no spot or wrinkle** or any such thing; but **that she would be holy and blameless**.*"

We are made holy and blameless, having no spot or wrinkle, because He has already cleansed us (past tense) by the washing of water with the word. The Greek word for "cleansed" is *katharizo*, which is from the same Greek word that Jesus used when He said that His word has made us "clean." In this Ephesians 5 passage, it says He has already cleansed the church by the washing of water with the *rhema*, the "right now, revelatory word proceeding from the mouth of God." It is from this experience that we are presented in all of our glory.

Let me tell you, when God spoke this word to me on my third visit out to the creek-bed altar, it became a *rhema* word that brought life to my heart. His spoken word is soothing and nurturing to the soul. It is a cleansing agent that washes away any impurity. I instantly felt clean inside-out. I can say that any time I have ever felt slimy from something I thought, believed, or did, the moment He would speak His living Word into my heart, I felt the glorious cleansing which washed through my entire being. Are you curious to know how thoroughly His spoken Word can actually cleanse you? Allow me to paint a picture.

Let's consider the capacity of the water that is stored inside His voice. Revelation 1:12-15 says, *"Then I turned to see the voice that was speaking with me...I saw one like a son of man...His head and His hair were white like white wool, like snow; and His eyes were like a flame of fire. His feet were like burnished bronze...and **His voice was like the sound of many waters**."* Imagine Jesus speaking His heart directly to you. Furthermore, imagine His words pouring over your soul with the force and magnitude of the Niagara Falls. That is the intensity of the water in His words! No doubt, you are definitely going to come out a clean and refreshed saint.

Amazingly, when Jesus said in John 15:2 that His Father prunes (or cleanses) us, it is so we may bear more fruit. There is no question that sin inhibits us from bearing good fruit. But because Jesus speaks His cleansing streams of life over us, we are pruned and prone to bear much fruit. *"I am the vine, you are the branches; he who abides in Me and I in him, he bears much fruit, for apart from Me you can do nothing"* (John 15:5). Every time we receive His *rhema* word, we are standing upstream in a river of living water, bathing and bearing abundant fruit in every season.

I must say, I was shocked that Jesus cleansed me of my sin before I ever got the chance to ask Him to forgive me. By the time those words could come out of my mouth, He told me He already had. Leave me out to dry? That is an understated opposite. I felt so clean and invigorated when I let Him pour the fountains of His goodness over my whole self. I was enlivened as He spoke into my inner man that I am clean, righteous, holy, blameless, and accepted in His sight.

This was the final lesson in my Rabbi's three-part revelatory teaching series about "His Instantaneous Mercy and Cleansing." These three revelations were now mine to own and utilize any time I found myself in a pickle. They were artillery with which I was sure to defeat the arch-enemies of Shame and Guilt.

There would be plenty of times to come when various forms of attack would confront me and try to take me back into that familiar prison of condemnation. But now I had the Word of God on my side, and it was truth that would never change. Never again would the devil be able to hold me down for too long without me knowing the truth that would set me free. No matter what, I am accepted by God, and His Word will always make me clean. He has already dealt with my sin on the cross, and all I need is to know what He has spoken: I am His beloved son in whom He is well-pleased!

A Guilt-Free Zone

There is no room for condemnation in the Kingdom of God. He is not judging us so He can bring us down in punishment for our wrongs. Jesus went as far as to say, "*For God did not send His Son into the world to condemn the world, but that the world through Him might be saved*" (John 3:17 NKJV). We who have been saved have absolutely no reason to fear punishment from God (see 1 John 4:18). Romans 8:1 says, "*Therefore there is now no condemnation for those who are in Christ Jesus.*" So if God is not bringing this kind of judgment upon us, why do we tend to do it to ourselves and others?

A lot of Christians humbly say, "I am a sinner saved by grace." This sounds good. You can look at yourself that way if you wish, but a higher perspective is the way God sees you. "*Our old self was crucified with Him, in order that our body of sin might be done away with, so that we would no longer be slaves to sin*" (Romans 6:6). The body of sin was crucified with Christ and no longer lives; thus you are no longer a slave to it. Since you were raised to newness of life with Christ, it is imperative that you "***consider yourselves*** *to be dead to sin, but alive to God in Christ Jesus*" (Romans 6:11). This is that whole renewal-of-the-mind thing. How you view yourself affects how you live and what level of victory you are able to maintain. "If you believe you are a sinner saved by grace, you will sin by faith"- Steve Backlund.

"*For sin shall not be master over you, for you are not under law but under grace*" (Romans 6:14). Paul has done a really good job of convincing me that I am no longer a sinner. I know that I still have the capacity to sin, and sometimes it still happens. However, it is not impossible to continue on with a sinless life either. Whatever hold sin used to have on my inner man has been demolished by the cross. It has been separated from my nature and put to death. It is not who I am. My new identity has no partnership with sin because identity was bestowed upon me from the Holy One in whom sin cannot exist.

I am not a sinner saved by grace. I used to be a sinner, but then I got saved by grace. Now I am a saint! It is not because of any heroic virtue, a series of posthumous miracles performed, or because I got on the pope's happy list. It is because I am a recipient of the gift of grace and an heir of the Kingdom of God. And so are you! If you read Romans 1:6-7, you will see that Paul declared the Christians to be saints because they are called of Jesus Christ and are beloved of God. It is that easy. The Greek word for "saint" is *hagios* and means "sacred (pure, blameless, consecrated), holy, saint." It is the same word that is translated "Holy," as in "Holy Spirit" and "The Holy One of God." The same sacred descriptions that we use for God are what He uses for us.

The Greek word for "sinner" is *hamartolos*. In the entire New Testament, this word is never used to describe a person who has truly embraced the effects of the cross and the resurrection. The only time *hamartolos* is somewhat mentioned in context to believers is in James 4:8 where it says, "*Draw near to God and He will draw near to you. Cleanse your hands, you sinners; and purify your hearts, you double-minded.*" But this was written to a group of people who were struggling with double-mindedness, trying to have the mind of Christ while still embracing Old Covenant mindsets. They wanted to live with one foot in and one foot out. Jesus calls this "lukewarm" in Revelation 3:15-16. Hopefully, they were inspired by James to become single-mindedly focused on the fullness of the grace of Christ, embracing sainthood through sonship and not works.

If you are interested in studying about our separation from *hamartolos*, perhaps you would enjoy reading Romans 5:8, Romans 5:19, Galatians 2:15-16, and 1 Timothy 1:15-16. (Please read the latter in context with the entire chapter.)

All through the New Testament we are referred to as saints, not as sinners. We would do ourselves a good service to stop referring to ourselves as "sinners saved by grace" and start declaring who we really are—saints. We are His beloved children, in whom He is well-pleased, the holy saints of God, perfected in holiness and blameless in His sight. That is the foundational starting point upon where our identity is built. From there is where each of our unique characters and personalities need to flow and be defined.

The Lord has started this new fad that has taken hold for about 2000 years now and doesn't seem to be letting up any time soon. It is the "in-thing" in His Kingdom to scout out people who are stuck in the mucky quicksand of condemnation and climb in there to pull them out. He then gives them a shower in His waterfalls of abounding grace and hands them a clean set of white robes and linens to wear. He always explains to the victim that the quicksand was not on His property because He would never own that type of landscaping. He tells them to "get up and sin no more." Then He commands a legion of His angels to escort them back to His land; and He never leaves their side.

Identity Theft

Seeing my dad dancing in the middle of a circle of pews in church was humiliating to my siblings and me. Jason, Amy, and I were very young back in the early 80's. I remember getting occasional glimpses of some peculiar behavior from my parents, Scott and Brenda, which I could not understand. They attempted to explain it to us in bite-sized pieces, but we just didn't quite get it. Every so often I would even hear them talking in some foreign language that I never knew they could speak. I wondered if they were able to communicate with our Turkish neighbors.

Different occurrences of bizarre behavior went on for a few years. And there was dad, yet again, jumping up in church during worship. He would dance around in the middle of that small, reverberant room. As he bounced and landed, the floor would shake the entire antique chapel. All of the pews were set in a circle, so whoever was in the middle had all eyes glued on them. I had never seen such conduct during sacred times, except on movies where Native Americans were doing ceremonial rain dances. I would be lying to say I was not thoroughly embarrassed. But I did not yet understand the side effects of the baptism in the Holy Spirit.

It was Dad and Charlene Robinson who were the ones to always draw such attention to themselves in Christ Fellowship Church. Occasionally, Charlene would blurt out some declaration in a foreign tongue, and moments later, Dad would burst out with an interpretation of the prophecy in English. When we got older, Dad would recall stories of that same period of time when he would cast demons out of people in the mental hospital where he worked. He was growing up into quite a mighty revivalist in those days. He was ahead of his time in that small church. Little did I know that Dad was a forerunner for a charismatic move of God that would later come to our church. Unfortunately, those glory days that we kids got to witness our parents living eventually came to a sad end, particularly for Dad.

Years later when I was in my mid-teens, I began having my own personal revival that changed my life. (You have read about the catalytic encounter that sparked this transformation in Chapter 4.) Once I discovered the baptism in the Holy Spirit and all the virtues that flow as a result, I began to recall the similar encounters of Mom and Dad. It became curious to me how such an accelerating adventure could have ever stalled for them.

Dad was always our greatest fan as my siblings and I were stepping into the deeper realms of God's glorious Kingdom. He was our biggest proponent when we looked for ways to minister to the world around us. He entrusted us into the care of our youth pastor as we were trained to be sold out to Jesus and to boldly proclaim our love for Him. Dad always promoted us to go all out for God.

But for some reason, it almost felt as if he was getting his spiritual fulfillment vicariously through us rather than from his own personal experiences. I had always carried a small vile of sorrow in my heart as I watched him having to live with the memory of the glory days of yesteryear. It seemed as if he had somewhere picked up a spirit of heaviness that weighed him down so much that he could no longer stand tall. I could never figure this out. What could have happened to put Dad in such a prison of condemnation that would restrain him from the glories he once tasted? Where had his faith and passion for his own personal revival gone?

A couple of years ago, Dad had an awakening and I finally learned the truth of how the devil found an open door to ambush him and rob him of his dignity. The devil blasted Dad with a deception grenade that knocked him off his rocker, and then he shackled him in the chains of unworthiness.

My dad used to be a very courageous man and was ready to step out boldly to do anything he thought he saw his Father in Heaven doing. He was not afraid of looking foolish in his obedience to God.

There was a couple in our church who had two little boys. The baby had a terminal illness and was not given very much time to live. Dad was so full of faith and had already seen God do miracles. He was rightly determined that God would continue to increase His power through him for signs and wonders. When he felt unction from the Holy Spirit, he stepped out and boldly proclaimed to this couple that their son's illness would not end in death. With full faith, they all trusted that a turn-around was imminent. Unfortunately, the turn-around never came, and the baby went on to be with the Lord. This was a devastating blow to all.

The baby's parents were obviously very grieved to lose their beloved son. Nonetheless, they were sweet-hearted people. They would have never blamed my dad or accused him as a false prophet. On the contrary, I believe that they appreciated Dad's comforting words and prayers as he brought them hope during a hard time.

The devil is of a different spirit though. He got right on his bullhorn and condemned Dad as a false prophet. He found him already on the ground in grief and kicked him while he was still down. In those days, it was common belief that if a person attempted to prophesy and their utterance did not happen exactly as stated, they were a false prophet. (It is Old Covenant to judge the prophet—see Deuteronomy 18:20-22; it is New Covenant to judge the prophecy rather than the person—see 1 Corinthians 14:29 in context with 1 Corinthians 13:9.)

Dad drank from this bitter cup of sorrow. He believed from then on that he was not worthy to attempt to prophesy again. He lost all of his stability and courage to be on the front line, leading his companions into the greater realms of glory. He lost credibility in his own eyes. He was under condemnation. And ever since then, he just stood behind his kids cheering us on to take the lead in our own unique roles while he remained hidden in the background. Many years went by with the memories of what had been.

System Recovery – Restore to an Earlier Date

Thankfully, the story does not end there. Over 20 years after that event came a new event of the redemptive kind. God always has a plan to redeem what the thief has stolen. A couple of years ago, Dad was speaking with our former pastor and one of my spiritual fathers, Bill Roberts. Bill was telling him about some radical revivalists from Bethel Church in Redding, California who were leading some meetings he had recently attended. Signs and wonders were happening right and left, and prophetic words were being dished out by the crate-full. God was moving and church members were being revitalized, energized, and ignited with fresh hope and faith to step out and walk in the power of God.

In the midst of all of that glory, the one thing that Pastor Bill was moved by the most was their freedom to fail. These revivalists were risk-takers and stepped out to try new things they had never done before. They had such confidence in the goodness of God that they were okay with trying to speak a prophetic word over someone that ended up being miles off. If they would pray for someone for a healing and they did not get healed, they were not discouraged but kept trying. "If at first you don't succeed, then try, try, again."

They taught the congregation that faith equals risk. If you never take risks, you will never see new results. The concept of risk inherently means there is a chance of failure; but it also means there is a chance of success. If you fall down trying, get back up and try again. If you make a mistake, learn from it and improve your technique.

God celebrates our risks above the results. He is just so happy that we step out and act like Jesus. The reason is because it is up to us whether or not we take the risk, but the results are up to Him. The only pressure we have is to give God the opportunity to do something profound, which is what He loves to do. The pressure for it to actually happen is all God's. And for the record, He is really good at His job. (This is the vantage point we at Bethel Church live by as we are learning to grow in the gifts of the Spirit. It works!)

This perspective on risk-taking was revelatory for Pastor Bill, and Dad was hearing it secondhand via Bill. Through the secondhand testimony, Dad's spiritually-blind eyes became instantly opened. He immediately was taken back in the spirit to the day his failed word fell to the ground as a seed planted into the soil of regret.

Jesus revealed to Dad that He is good and actually loves the fact that Dad took the risk and stepped out to speak such a bold word to that family. The word may not have been right, but the heart behind it was. Dad learned that there is a freedom to fail in his attempts to take risks, and that the reward is not in the result but in the faith. For the first time, he understood that the past twenty-plus years had been robbed from him and that he never needed to shrink back for one second.

"You will know the truth, and the truth will make you free" (John 8:32). Dad now understood the truth. In the blink of an eye, he broke free from the shackles of condemnation. All of that time, God was proud of what he had done—not ashamed.

Since that day of redemption, Dad has become a different man. Well, different from whom I had known nearly all of my life. The Lord took him back to the point where he lost his dignity and restored it back to him. He picked up right where he left off as though it was just a wrinkle in time.

It was only the next day when he and Mom went into Wal-Mart on their way home from church and discovered that God had gone shopping with them. While they were walking in the soda aisle, a mentally handicapped man and his wife came up to them and started staring at them while mumbling. Not being able to understand his slurred and incoherent speech, Dad found his heart welling up with compassion. An old familiar authority began resurfacing to the point where he could not refrain from putting his hand on this man's shoulder. Dad just stared into the man's eyes as he was flowing with mercy. The glory of God immediately surrounded all four of them.

Then the most unusual and unexpected thing happened. The man's speech instantly became clear and sensible. While Dad was touching him, they held an intelligent conversation and he was able to bless him and his wife. Then when his hand came off of the shoulder, the man immediately went right back into incoherency again. Three or four times, Dad did this with the same results. There was something about the touch that brought a sense of abundant life that was lacking otherwise. It was supernatural. Other bystanders also noticed this.

After Mom and Dad exited the store, that couple was leaving just behind them. Dad did not feel settled that God was finished yet; so he turned and asked the man if he had anything physically wrong with him. Speaking coherently on his own at this point, he explained that he had a torn rotator cuff and could not afford surgery. Dad asked if he could pray for a healing and the man permitted.

Mom and Dad invited the presence of Jesus to come and they laid hands on him. As anybody should do in the presence of the Almighty, Dad asked the man to lift his hands to the Lord. He followed suit and was shocked to discover that his arms lifted all the way, which was impossible to do with the injury. Dad asked him to do things he could not do. He started doing windmills with his arm. It was a miracle before their eyes. It was a sneak-attack glory encounter for all involved.

This is just one story of many glory encounters that have happened to Mom and Dad since his revelatory breakthrough. God truly is restoring everything the locusts have eaten, one by one. There is no room for guilt and condemnation in the Kingdom of God.

The Fraudulent Plaintiff

The source of condemnation never has any connection to God. It is strictly the work of the devil. His name is "the Accuser of the Brethren" (see Revelation 12:10). He is the one who is watching for any sign of imperfection for which to put us on trial. If he can find a weak spot in the fabric of our faith, he will rip it to shreds, causing us to lose sight of our enduring freedom. He will shame a person into a state of self-containment, condemning him as a sinner who deserves time and distance away from the presence of our Savior.

But that is a paradox. Jesus is our Savior for the very purpose of getting us into His presence in spite of our sins. He does not accept us with our sins; He accepts us separate from our sins. He separates us from our sins, accepting us purely. Regardless of what the accuser wants to remind us about from our past (spanning from years ago to seconds ago), Jesus is the Truth, and when you know the truth, the Truth will make you free.

God becomes grieved when we clothe ourselves in a straitjacket of guilt derived from the belief that it is our deserved lot. God is not issuing restraining orders or probationary periods from His presence to His children. So many people believe lies of this magnitude and withdraw from a close relationship with God or anything pertaining to Him. Oftentimes, months, years, and even lifetimes go by with the memory of an intimate God they once knew, but the hounding sentence of guilt for a wrong once done keeps them constrained in their lonely state. That condition can cause additional sinful fruits to spring forth, just adding to the increasing sense of guilt. Maybe you have experienced that at one point or another and can identify. Please know that the bad fruit is not nearly the problem that isolation is. Take care of the root issue and the rest gets resolved.

I recently visited my chiropractor, Dr. Todd Royse. He is an excellent doctor and a mighty revivalist who is bringing the Kingdom of God into the health arena. He was sharing with me a story about his dad.

When his dad was around 13 years old, he and his entire family were hardworking farmers, putting in 16-hour days, seven days a week, just barely scraping by financially. Their hearts were in church, but they could only attend on rare times between seasons. One Sunday after harvest had let up, he and his twin brother finally had the opportunity to pay a visit to their local church. They probably went feeling good about themselves for being respectful to the house of God. When the preacher noticed them sitting there, he called out in a loud, thundering voice, "Look, here are the backsliders!" It is not difficult to imagine how this must have felt. Damaged in the heart, that was the last time Dr. Todd's dad went to church for several decades.

All of those years, he avoided anything pertaining to God up until about 10 years ago when he had a near death experience after overdosing on alcohol. I can't help but wonder if he would have ever developed this type of lifestyle if he would have been received by that church in his youth. In his sickly condition, Dr. Todd had the privilege of leading him back to the Lord.

How many people are out there who have been condemned either by religion, the world, or by themselves for things done that were ungodly or simply imperfect? It is very easy to withdraw from God in guilt and shame, believing that is what we deserve.

We all face opportunities to give in to this kind of deception. That is why it is important to know the truth of who we are to God. God does not judge us like that. He does not want us wasting precious moments of life in that prison when we could be enjoying the bounty of life with Him. Although God is the One who restores the years the locusts have stolen (see Joel 2:25), He much prefers that we never let the locusts steal from us in the first place. Those are years that we could be growing into greater realms of intimacy in the glory of God. He is the Redeemer and Healer of brokenness. However, He knows we are much better off if we do not lose things from the front end at all. It is not necessary to go through those seasons of despair for anyone who lives in their true identity and does not weaken under the pressures of the deceiver.

When the accuser accuses us of what we have done, we must remind ourselves of what Jesus has done. He has done everything necessary for us to live freely and successfully in His presence regardless of our circumstances, and **it is finished**. As far as God is concerned, we are still His princes and princesses. We must do everything we can to remember who we are when we face the opportunity to shrink back into the realm of lost time. Then we can bypass it and thrive without missing a beat.

12

Scrutinize Jesus Instead

One important lesson I have been learning over the years is the vitality of Colossians 3:2: "*Set your mind on the things above, not on the things that are on earth.*" No matter what situation or circumstance is pressing, it is crucial that we never lose sight of our Lord and Savior in Heaven. Even when we have sinned, we have a choice of where we will place our attention—on the sin or on Christ. One option is to keep our focus on the sin: either in pleasure that keeps it fueled, or in resistance, trying our hardest to get clean of it and stay out of it.

Believe it or not, neither option is actually a worse scenario than the other. It seems worse to keep your eyes on a sin that you intend to continue in than it does to keep your eyes on a sin from which you are trying to defend yourself. But each problem is actually one and the same when you get down to it. The issue is not so much whether you prefer the sin or not, but the simple fact that you are giving your attention to sin rather than to Jesus. It is setting your mind on things of the Earth, not on the things above. What we most give our attention to is what most empowers us, and it will directly affect the end result every time. The better option is to place our attention on the things above, namely Jesus.

In John 15, Jesus is teaching us a very important lesson that actually can include overcoming sin. John 15:5 says, "*I am the vine, you are the branches; he who abides in Me and I in him, he bears much fruit, for apart from Me you can do nothing.*" It is impossible to overcome sin in your own strength. Cleansing from sin can only happen because He has made us clean. In this case, cleansing comes from His spoken word. (See John 15:3. Refer also to the *Don't Call Unclean What I Have Called Clean* section of Chapter 10.)

If you want to break a sin pattern, you must stop paying all of your attention to the sin because then you are on your own. Rather, put your attention on the One who is inviting you to abide in Him. In doing so, it brings you into the awareness that He also abides in you and causes you to bear the good fruit.

Galatians 5 teaches us that when we are living by the Holy Spirit, we will not sin; but instead, we will bear much good fruit. Conversely, when we are not walking in relationship with the Holy Spirit, we are living by our own strength and will, by default, produce a whole lot of bad fruit. Apart from God, we can do nothing that is worthwhile to His Kingdom. The choice is obvious and simple: do your own thing and fail in your attempts to overcome sin; or live in intimate, restful union with the Tree of Life (Jesus), and His fruit and purity will become your natural by-products.

God's bounty of love disarms sin and crowds it out of the space it once occupied. If it doesn't, then you haven't yet experienced the power of His love the way He wants you to. When you encounter the glorious, ecstatic presence of the Lover of Our Souls, even the memory of sin's dark existence disappears the same way as the night stars do in the rising of the Morning Star. If sin is not set before you any longer, you will surely not commit it. Where will you choose to set your affections?

Lovingkindness

Jesus loves us so much more than we think, even when we are in the thick of sin. His disposition toward us will never be moved even by an inch, no matter what horrible crimes we may commit.

Psalm 33:5 says, "*He loves righteousness and justice; the earth is full of the lovingkindness of the Lord.*" The Old Testament is chock-full of verses that speak of the lovingkindness of the Lord. One that we are all probably familiar with is in the Shepherd's chapter. Psalm 23:6

says, "*Surely goodness and lovingkindness will follow me all the days of my life, and I will dwell in the house of the Lord forever.*" Some versions often will translate *lovingkindness* as *mercy*. The Hebrew word for it is actually *hesed* (or *chesed*). This word has a much deeper meaning than the poetic sound of "lovingkindness," although it includes the virtues of love and kindness.

In brief, *hesed* actually is referring to the covenant-loyalty love of God. It is a term that is referring to the fact that He has made a covenant to love and take complete care of His people as our Father on unconditional terms. A covenant is a pact that is eternally binding, and the only legal way out is by death. If a covenant is broken, death by punishment is imminent.

The Old Covenant was fulfilled by Jesus and then became null and void because of His death. But God made a New Covenant of eternal and infinite proportions; and since Jesus has died once for all and never again, this covenant is eternally binding. He will not break His covenant. He has sworn to us that He will die before He would go against His promise. He is true to His word. He is abundantly full of *hesed* for us. He is loyal to His covenant to love us as His children and take complete care of us always, forgiving us thoroughly of every single sin and remembering them no more. This cannot be shaken no matter what we may do.

In the New Testament, there is a Greek word that replaces the Hebrew word *hesed*. It is the word *agapao*, or *agape*. This word carries the same weight as *hesed* and usually is defined as "unconditional love." You see, God has covenanted that He will love us no matter what happens. It is absolutely impossible to get God to love you any more or any less than He already does. You cannot fluctuate an infinite virtue. This is why Paul said, "*For I am convinced that neither death, nor life, nor angels, nor principalities, nor things present, nor things to come, nor powers, nor height, nor depth, nor any other created thing, will be able to separate us from the love* (agape) *of God, which is in Christ Jesus our Lord*" (Romans 8:38-39).

It is love in covenant.

Look at Psalm 33:5 again, "*He loves righteousness and justice; the earth is full of the lovingkindness of the Lord.*" It is interesting that He mentions loving righteousness and justice in the same breath as filling the Earth with His covenant-loyalty love.

In the most famous memory verse ever quoted, Jesus actually stated this same truth in light of the terms of the New Covenant. "*For God so loved* (agapao) *the world, that He gave His only begotten Son, that whoever believes in Him shall not perish, but have eternal life*" (John 3:16). The righteousness and justice of God was fulfilled in the Son being given as the sacrifice that provides us with eternal life. This happened because God so unconditionally loved the world. He fills the Earth with His covenant-loyalty, unconditional love, and this includes filling you, me, and our neighbors.

Jesus said that God so *agapao's* the world that He would go as far as to sacrifice His only beloved Son so that we could have eternal life. He was well aware of the fact that we were all once living in our rebellious sins separate from Him. But our filth was not what He was fixated upon. He was looking past the evil intentions of our hearts into our empty, lost souls with the sentimental memories of how things were back before our species fell away from the glory.

He did not look upon us with anger or judgment, but with compassion and generosity. "*For God did not send the Son into the world to judge the world, but that the world might be saved through Him*" (John 3:17). As I said before, Jesus loves us so much more than we think, even when we are in the thick of sin. Romans 5:8 says, "*But God demonstrates His own love toward us, in that while we were yet sinners, Christ died for us.*" In the same speech where Jesus introduced the legendary John 3:16, He also revealed a key to how we can deal with sin when it ambushes us from every direction.

The Serpent's Rod

The two verses prior hide a golden key within them. It must be uncovered for us to find His provision to victory in the time of overwhelming vulnerability to sin and temptation. Jesus said, "*As Moses lifted up the serpent in the wilderness, even so must the Son of*

Man be lifted up; so that whoever believes will in Him have eternal life" (John 3:14-15). It is obvious that Jesus was referring to the type of death He would eventually face when lifted up on the cross, a death that would provide for our eternal salvation. Of all the examples to use, why did He feel He needed to compare it to Moses lifting up a serpent in the wilderness? Don't serpents represent the devil and evil things?

To understand the full concept of what Jesus was conveying, we need to take a look at the actual story where Moses lifted up a serpent in the wilderness. It is in Numbers 21. It begins with Israel journeying through the desert towards the Promised Land and running into some unexpected trouble. On several occasions, the nearby nations would rise up against God's people along the way because they did not want them crossing through their land. This time, a Canaanite king of Arad brought a fight to them and was actually successful in taking some of them captive.

Israel pleaded with God to deliver their enemy into their hand, and He saw to it. They went to war, slaughtering the whole land of Arad.

After this amazing defeat that the Lord provided for them, they quickly forgot of His goodness, yet again, once they got back to their long, boring journey through the desert. They had their high in the heat of the moment when God revealed His might. Unfortunately, they never learned how to steward their loyal devotion to love Him in the daily rhythms of life.

Getting back to the wilderness journey after that excitement was probably comparable to a quick transition from the adrenaline rush of watching *Gladiator* to rushing home so you can hash out your annual itemized taxes. What a downer! That was only the case for the Israelites, however, because they had never tasted the goodness of the inner caverns of God's heart, which was open for their exploration at any moment they desired.

These thrill-seekers were heartless in their relation to God and relentless in their expressions of selfishness and greed. Forgetting the slavery and torture they formerly suffered in Egypt and their cries to

God for deliverance years ago, they felt the need to speak out against God. They grumbled about the temporary inconveniences of the passageway to their Promised Land. After this great deliverance (as well as many others), they went as far as to actually say that God brought them out there to let them die in the wilderness. To spread some icing on their dump cake, they even told Him how much they loathed the food that He had been miraculously and lovingly providing for them.

Can you imagine the smack in the face this must have been to God? They were selfish, evil-hearted people who lived for the moment. They did not understand that longsuffering is actually a virtue that promises really good rewards for those who can wait. These people just could not wait. Because their evil hearts were full of impatience and dissatisfaction in the Lord, what should have only been a couple of weeks of inconvenience in the desert turned into 40 long years. The toil and pain of life in the wilderness was actually brought upon by themselves.

Turning the Tables

This particular incident was a unique one of many. God got fed up with His people's arrogance and disrespect. Numbers 21:6 says, "*The Lord sent fiery serpents among the people and they bit the people, so that many people of Israel died.*" It was high time that the sins of the people came back and bit them in the butt. People were dying right and left throughout the camp. Because the people's hearts were so hard and stubborn, God knew it would take something of such dramatic measure to awaken them to the reality of their state of sinfulness and separation. That is exactly what it did.

Numbers 21:7 tells how they went to Moses confessing their sins of speaking bitterly against God and him. They pleaded with him saying, "*Intercede with the Lord, that He may remove the serpents from us.*" Moses was the most humble man in all the Earth (says Numbers 12:3) and put his own hurt feelings aside in compassion for his people. God is even more humble and compassionate than Moses. When Moses spoke to God, He always listened. So he prayed to the Lord for mercy.

Numbers 21:8-9 says, *"Then the Lord said to Moses, 'Make a fiery serpent, and set it on a standard* (a staff); *and it shall come about, that everyone who is bitten, when he looks at it, he will live.' And Moses made a bronze serpent and set it on the standard; and it came about, that if a serpent bit any man, when he looked to the bronze serpent, he lived."* Notice something here. The people pleaded for God to remove the serpents from them so they would not die. God intervened, but He did not do it the way they requested (as He often doesn't). Instead of removing the serpents from their midst, He created an opportunity that would overpower the snakebites and render them harmless.

My mental image of this scene is when Indiana Jones, in the *Raiders of the Lost Ark*, was trapped in the ancient Egyptian tomb surrounded by thousands of snakes. There was no way to avoid stepping on some here and there. Dr. Jones and Marion were treading very lightly and carefully, and luckily they never got bitten. They were only two people in a big, open room. Imagine an area the size of a small city being filled with millions of slithering, angry snakes on the prowl, with no space to maneuver around them. Consider a multitude of probably over a million people crowded together wanting to get around the snakes but stepping all over them in their attempt. Those people wouldn't stand much of a chance.

It would probably look a lot like a giant mosh pit. They would all be jumping around and screaming in a stampede as they tried to dodge the innumerable piles of vipers striking at their legs. The chaotic movement and commotion would agitate the snakes all the more as they sensed fear in the atmosphere. In this hazardous predicament, there would only be one direction I would want to turn my attention to, and that is down. I would want to keep my eyes on the striker because one second of blinking or looking the other way could mean instant death from any direction.

So why wouldn't God just remove the snakes from them? Because He was testing the faith of His people. Would they continue to put their trust in their own ability to avoid the strike of the serpent? They might be able to dodge a few of them, but they surely would not last for long. God created a dilemma for them that they had no time to solve.

The split-second choice the people had to make was whether they would risk trusting in God's peculiar provision that made no sense, or to rely on their own mongoose reflexes to take these snakes on by themselves. It would require a lot of risky faith to take your eyes off of the company of vipers that are taking stance beside you in order to look up at a bronze-casted statue of a fiery serpent on the hill. You would need much faith to believe that it could produce a greater result than you could.

The craziest part of this ordeal is that their obedience did not ensure that they would not get bitten. God said, "*It shall come about, that everyone who is bitten, when he looks at it, he will live.*" Miraculously, everyone who was bitten that looked up at Moses' serpent on a pole was saved, and they did not die from the snakebites they took.

Jesus, the Other Kind of Serpent

This is a profound story that Jesus briefly wove into His message when He said, "*As Moses lifted up the serpent in the wilderness, even so must the Son of Man be lifted up; so that whoever believes will in Him have eternal life*" (John 3:14-15). The serpents that were striking the children of God represented their sin. It is not to say that God sent sin upon them; but He sent the repercussions of their sin upon them, for the wages of sin is death (Romans 6:23). Interestingly, the very provision that God made for their salvation from the sting of the poisonous serpents was an image of the very thing killing them. Although the statue looked like a serpent, it was not of the same nature and contained no venom. It contained the power for life.

It is a parallel of what Jesus became for those of us who have also felt (and still do at times) the sting of our sins. Jesus was lifted up on the cross on the hill of Calvary. When we are surrounded by sins and temptations and are being bitten by them, we are brought into the same dilemma. Will we risk trusting in God's peculiar provision that is often underestimated, or will we rely on our own mongoose reflexes to take our sins on by ourselves? It is common instinct to put all focus upon the sin at hand and try to overcome it by intense focus and sheer willpower. But Jesus is letting us in on the secret that trying to do so will only cause us to get bitten. It can be a lethal option.

Jesus is like that fiery serpent on the rod due to the fact that He became the very thing that was killing us. "*He (God) made Him (Jesus) who knew no sin to be sin on our behalf, so that we might become the righteousness of God in Him*" (2 Corinthians 5:21). Of course, Jesus has never sinned one time. But He became our substitute for sin and punishment. **He became sin** upon the cross so that we could become the righteousness of God in Him. What a trade!

Furthermore, "*Christ redeemed us from the curse of the Law, having become a curse for us*" (Galatians 3:13). So, on the cross, He became sin to break the power of sin off of us, and He became a curse to break the curse of sin and death off of us. There is no curse of any form that has any power over a child of the Most High God if we can believe the full reality of what He has done for us on the cross. He became the fiery serpent lifted up that saves all who would look away from the sting of sin and up to Him.

Climbing Out of Sin

If you are ever struggling in a sin or a weakness and are having difficulty shaking it, it is crucial to remove your focus from the problem and lift up your eyes to Jesus. You may be standing smack dab in the middle of it and cannot see anything but sin for miles in every direction with no way through it. I don't care if you have barely slipped into some minute issue that you've never before struggled with, or if you committed the worst sin you could dream up and have tried to repent of 10 different occurrences of it in the last three days. The Lord is asking you to lift your eyes off of the sin and fix them onto Jesus. Stop looking at your problem and start looking at your solution.

You are already incapable of conquering this battle on your own strength and wisdom. Jesus is your only way of escape, and His arms are spread wide with an open invitation for you to draw near immediately. God's provision of salvation from the deadly snakebites was delivered even after they had been bitten and were still getting bitten by all the snakes surrounding them. The issue was no longer about the snakes and the sins that invited them; it shifted to the provision of God.

God is very eager to lead us away from focusing on our problems to focusing on the solution—His Son. It is time that we learn to lift our attention upward to give our great Deliverer the opportunity to do what He is bent on doing. To God, sin is not the issue anymore; abundant life is His issue, and that's where He wants us to focus intently, regardless of what our circumstance is. It makes no difference where you are in life or what condition you are in; Calvary Hill is always in view with Jesus standing there, already crucified, and fully resurrected. He is the Serpent on the Rod who became sin to make us righteous. He will accept you no matter your condition. All you have to do is lift your eyes up to Him and take the risk of trusting that He can render the power of sin powerless in your life.

What you set your attention on is what will empower you. If you set your attention on the sin, it will be the sin that continues to feed you strength. If you set it on Jesus, He will empower you in righteousness. Romans 8:37 says, *"But in all these things we overwhelmingly conquer through Him who loved us."* It is not by your own strength that you can conquer anything, but only through encountering His love.

I have personally learned that if I fall into a sin, I have the opportunity to promptly look up to Him for help. I have the choice of whether to stew in the sin and try to find my own way out of it, or to do rapid repentance and be quickly restored into intimacy with Jesus. I am a fan of rapid repentance. He is so accepting of anyone who will just lift their eyes to Him. I can tread in any direction and find no relief from sin or temptation. But when I look up and behold the Lamb of God who has taken away the sins of the world, He is reaching His hand out to lift me right back to the place where I belong—in His holy presence. It is that easy.

He truly has a seat reserved for us in the heavenly places that is above all of the muck of this world. It is the place where victory and purity are derived. Everything inferior is below and far removed under the feet of those who are seated there. We can dwell there.

Winning in Temptation

The bonus about this truth of the serpent's rod is that it works with temptation as well. I believe it is possible to live in such a way that temptation can virtually be averted and avoided much more often than you and I may currently experience. If it were not possible, I don't believe Jesus would have taught us to pray for it. *"Do not lead us into temptation, but deliver us from evil"* (Matthew 6:13). But until we learn to live every moment of our lives in the elevated position He is training us for, we will get tempted at times.

Temptation is not an indication that there is anything wrong with you. It is not a sin. Temptation is when someone (visible or invisible) tries to lure you into doing something that you should not do. Jesus never sinned, but even He was tempted in all ways (see Hebrews 4:15).

Sometimes the enemy brings a heavy ambush and dramatically heightens the enticements that he knows we may be susceptible to. These are moments that we must be well prepared to handle. The way to conquer this is not to put your dukes up and try to win the battle with your own strength and wits. That may work for a season, but it will not be too long before you will eventually crumble. Jesus has given us authority over the devil and we can rebuke him or the temptation and command him to leave us, and we should. I do. But I don't spend too long there. Jesus is looking for us to look to Him in these times, not the problems. Our victory comes from Him, not ourselves.

When faced with an opportunity to partake of a sin that looks really good in the moment, the best way out is to simply look to the Lord and shift your affections to Him. Obviously that is easier said than done. I have found that some of my most beautiful moments of worship were when I faced the greatest temptations and chose to adore Him above the opportunity that was knocking. This is a sacrifice with a pleasant aroma to God.

No temptation has overtaken you but such as is common to man; and God is faithful, who will not allow you to be tempted beyond what you are able, but with the temptation will provide the way of escape also, so that you will be able to endure it (1 Corinthians 10:13).

God is not waiting for us to find our own way out of our sins and temptations. **He is the Way**. It is all about where we are setting our eyes. Where we fix our attention is where we will end up. God does not pull out His whip on us for making bad choices in life. He is calling on us to lay the failures aside and fix our eyes on Him. As we run towards Him, He takes care of all of the peripheral problems.

*Therefore, since we have so great a cloud of witnesses surrounding us, let us also lay aside every encumbrance and the sin which so easily entangles us, and let us run with endurance the race that is set before us, **fixing our eyes on Jesus**, the author and perfecter of faith, who for the joy set before Him endured the cross, despising the shame, and has sat down at the right hand of the throne of God* (Hebrews 12:1-2).

Grace is About More Than Sin

God's goal is not to get us clean. That is just the starting point. He is actually trying to make us super powerful and free children of God. Grace doesn't only love us when we don't deserve it; it empowers us to be able to live lives that demonstrate what it is to be a carrier of the glory of God. Grace empowers righteousness and supernatural living. God is not trying to get us to the place where we have finally conquered a trek to the summit of our sins and weaknesses so we can plant our victory flag. His goal is to elevate us beyond that into a realm that is far above anything earthly, where we can enjoy the ecstasies of His glorious presence.

Jesus was able to overcome all trials of life by meditating on His Father and on His reinstatement to the right hand of the throne of God in Heaven. And now we know that God has *"raised us up with Him, and seated us with Him in the heavenly places in Christ Jesus"*

(Ephesians 2:6). This is the place we have already been seated. Setting our minds on Christ in this place ensures us victory over trials and brings us into the abiding reality of Heaven. It is a place where we can experience the bliss of the vibrant glory of the Lord. It is where we can draw our strength from the Tree of Life which is planted in the Paradise of God (see Revelation 2:7). It is from this place that we receive what the New Testament refers to as the true Sabbath rest, which we are all called into. That is where we are headed next.

13

The Striving to Rest Paradox

God has opened the door to Heaven and given everyone the standing invitation to come enjoy the bounty of His goodness. He has made His glory available for all to revel in. He is delighted for us to make it our sole ambition to not only taste of this through a momentary encounter, but to abide there daily. He is calling us all to enter into His Sabbath rest.

What is this Sabbath rest? It is a state of being where we get to peacefully rest from the burdens of life in the fullness of the presence of God and enjoy the abundance of His glorious love in all ways. It is from this place that we learn how to make the Earth around us look like Heaven through a strength that is not our own.

So how do we enter into that place of euphoric rest in the vivacious glory of God? That is the question of the ages. It is what everyone is searching for in some fashion or another. It is a promise from God for all who believe. As a matter of fact, it is a command for us to make every effort to enter that rest.

Hebrews 4:11 says, *"Therefore let us be diligent to enter that rest, so that no one will fall, through following the same example of disobedience."* We as Christians have the tendency to work so hard to keep ourselves from falling. However, this verse is a directive to do the opposite and actually stop working so hard. It says that **rest** will keep us from falling.

Just before this, Hebrews 4:10 says, *"For the one who has entered His rest has himself also rested from his works, as God did from His."* Just as Ephesians 2:8-9 promises that our salvation is not a result of works, but of grace through faith, so does the promise of our protection from falling come through resting from our works. We, in all of our strength, are incapable of keeping ourselves from falling, no matter how hard we try. So maybe we should move on to another method for success.

In a close look at Hebrews, chapters 3 and 4, God's focus is actually not so much on the falling-factor as it is on the rest-factor. God so deeply wants us all to enter into this promised rest. If this passage is telling us of our need for rest, then it surely will also explain how we can achieve it. So let's take this journey through Hebrews 4:11-16 along the trail God has blazed, which leads to the Sabbath rest.

Naked at the trailhead

For the word of God is living and active and sharper than any two-edged sword, and piercing as far as the division of soul and spirit, of both joints and marrow, and able to judge the thoughts and intentions of the heart. And there is no creature hidden from His sight, but all things are open and laid bare to the eyes of Him with whom we have to do (Hebrews 4:12-13).

Now, I'll say what many people have probably thought and didn't have the nerve to say out loud: What in God's name do these two verses have anything to do with the prior ones about Sabbath rest?

I used to assume that Hebrews 4:11 is the ending of one thought and subsection, making Hebrews 4:12 the beginning of a new one. After all, it usually comes with its own subtitle. It would make it easier to read not having to figure out a flow of thought. The problem with that idea is that verse 12 begins with the word *for*, which is a connector-word bridging what precedes it with what follows it. Because it is a connector that demands a flow, we can conclude that the answer for how to enter that promised rest is surely on its way.

Consider the idea of being diligent to enter into the tranquil, spiritual Sabbath rest of God. Doesn't it sound wonderfully desirable? Now hold that concept next to the thought of God's sharp sword piercing into the deepest recesses of your heart, exposing every thought and intention that is hidden deep within you so He can bring them under judgment. I'm sorry, but this sounds to me like a contradiction of terms and a cruel joke.

God is essentially saying, "You go ahead and rest while I shove this blazing sword into your chest so I can inspect the concealed thoughts and motives of your heart. Let me fillet your heart and mind to see what it is stuffed full with. But you just relax and rest." How am I supposed to be calmed when I know He is sticking my heart with a blade? Even worse, how am I supposed to rest when I know that He is scrutinizing all of the secrets I keep hidden inside of my heart? He might discover who I really am down in there and realize that He is not as happy with me as we all wanted to believe.

This scenario reminds me of a story about a young redneck gentleman who really wanted to marry his sweetheart who he had already been in love with for a couple of years. So he did the chivalrous thing by visiting with her redneck father in order to ask for her hand in marriage. Her dad knew he would be coming over and accurately suspected the reason; so he waited patiently for him, sitting in his living room recliner with a Coke in one hand and a shotgun in the other. He didn't intend to shoot the young guy but was just secretly having fun intimidating him.

Let's pretend he told the young man to relax while he interrogated him for every secret thing he had ever done. There is nothing relaxing about having a loaded shotgun pointed at your chest while having to tell your secrets to the person who will cringe at them the most.

That is how this order of sequences can feel when we reach the point of utmost vulnerability before the Lord. Thankfully, we have a God whose motive is not the same as the redneck with the shotgun. He never does anything to frighten or belittle us. He *does* have a sword, and He *does* use it to pierce our souls and spirits. He *is* inspecting our inner hearts. However, His Word is a love sword, and it only hurts the parts that we're not ready to surrender to Him. But to the yielded, His Word is Spirit and Life (see John 6:63).

It is His spoken Word (Greek: *Logos*) that is sharper than a two-edged sword which divides soul and spirit, joint and marrow. When He speaks to us, He declares over us who we truly are; and He separates us from who we are not. He's calling you and me a child of the Most High God. With His sword, He is separating from us all the things that are not of Him, and neither are they part of our true divine nature. The only pain that comes in this surgery is from the parts of our old identity that we continue clutching while He is cutting. But in selfless surrender, this surgery actually brings deep inner healing. It's like getting a big, ugly tumor cut out that obviously never belonged there in the first place.

The Lord is calling on us to be transparent before Him, regardless of what lies beneath the surface. He can already see every little detail hidden inside each of our hearts, thoughts, and intentions. He sees the ugly and the beautiful. There is nothing that is hidden from His sight, so we may as well not try to cover it up. He desires to find no gap between what He sees within us and what we are willing to own up to. Yes, it is true that we are all weak in and of ourselves. If we don't admit this, we are the only ones fooled.

When the Lord exposes to us where we are weak, we need to learn to acknowledge it to Him openly. It is certainly a painful experience to look at weakness and admit to it; but transparency is the beginning of a necessary healing.

Fig Leaf Fantasies

Hiding is not a good option. Adam and Eve hid behind God's fig leaf because they were ashamed of what He would see. Sometimes we hide behind the things of God. Sometimes we even try to hide from God altogether. It is easier to cover up our weaknesses by being noticed for the things that make us appear strong than it is to be true to ourselves and face the fact that we have issues. That is when we try to secure our identity in false places.

A pastor can feel good about preaching in a pulpit before a crowd of thousands every week as the congregation revels in his amazing Bible teachings; and yet he is secretly agonizing over a porn-addiction. A person can build a company from ground up and be the most cutting edge CEO and local public figure; and yet he dreads going home every evening because he doesn't know how to make his wife feel treasured. Someone can be the greatest Christian singer/songwriter the industry has lobbed onto the stage; and after the roaring crowd disperses, she sinks back into a lonely depression until the next fix of shallow, fanatical affirmations.

There are countless things we can use to masquerade our true selves. And somehow we think if we can fool our friends, we might also be fooling God. But God's eyesight is sharper than even Superman's. Lead cannot block it, and neither can fig leaves. *"All things are open and laid bare to the eyes of Him with whom we have to do"* (Hebrews 4:13).

God is not looking for falsified identities or avatars that present a strength or beauty that does not originate from the core of who you are. Jesus wants you and He wants who you are, as is. There are too many Davids running around trying to fill out Saul's armor while God intends to advance them through their own unique set of strengths. When we try to be someone we are not, it ends up looking very fake and weak. It carries no value or weight with God. It is what He classifies as works built by wood, hay, and straw whose quality will be tested with fire. *"If any man's work is burned up, he will suffer loss; but he himself will be saved, yet so as through fire"* (1 Corinthians 3:15).

It is not to say that God is bringing wrath upon the people who are living like this. Salvation is still completely for them. It is just to say that God can't bless what He didn't bestow upon a person. So we need to let Him trim off the fat of falsehood and get down to the leanness of our true inner selves. Jesus accepts us as we are, and He wants us to accept ourselves as we are, warts and beauty marks. God wants us to be naked and not ashamed. If the Lord has been revealing to you an area of weakness in your life that you have been ignoring, perhaps it is time to own up to it and acknowledge it to Him. It is called confession. It is healthy. Openly acknowledging our condition to God is the first step onto the pathway towards His Sabbath rest.

Been There, Done That…
Well, Been There At Least

The next leg of this journey is to recognize the perspective of Christ in this matter. Hebrews 4:14-15 goes on to say, *"Therefore, since we have a great high priest who has passed through the heavens, Jesus the Son of God, let us hold fast our confession. For we do not have a high priest who cannot sympathize with our weaknesses, but One who has been tempted in all things as we are, yet without sin."*

This passage explains that Jesus is our Great High Priest, and because He has been tempted in all things just the same as us, He understands what it feels like to have weaknesses. He never fell to sin under temptation, but He definitely considered it or it would not have been legitimate temptation. Because of this truth, Jesus is common to us in that way. Let it be known, He does not hold over our heads the fact that He succeeded and we are failures because we didn't. Rather, He identifies with us and sympathizes with us in our weaknesses. He has compassion in the midst of our frailty.

Jesus is our Great High Priest. He is the one and only remaining high priest forever. He stands before the mercy seat of God on our behalf, making intercession for us continually. He has taken the blood of His sacrifice before God, and it has cleansed us of all our junk. *"How much more will the blood of Christ, who through the eternal Spirit offered Himself without blemish to God, cleanse your conscience from dead works to serve the living God?"* (Hebrews 9:14). He stands in the gap for us and has actually become the bridge that connects us back to God. He is quick to forgive and instant to restore.

We must stop trying to hide our weaknesses behind fig leaves. We try so hard to be perfect. But Jesus said, *"Come to Me, all who are weary and heavy-laden, and I will give you rest"* (Matthew 11:28). He said, *"If anyone is thirsty, let him come to Me and drink"* (John 7:37). He also said, *"It is not those who are healthy who need a physician, but those who are sick; I did not come to call the righteous, but sinners"* (Mark 2:17). Notice that Jesus is always looking for and reaching out to imperfect people who are stuck in weak spots.

He is inviting us in our current condition, strong or weak, into an encounter with Himself. Even in our weakness, He invites us in. Jesus' name is the Door (see John 10:7). He is an ever-open door, and whatever God has opened no man can shut (see Revelation 3:8). Whatever your condition, accept His unconditionally-loving invitation and enter in. And no matter what, come as you are.

Understood, Sympathized, Released

There was a time when my wife, Jessica, and I were dealing with some stress in our relationship. For about three days we were reacting to each other in ways no spouse ought to. There were a few issues that had been coming at us, and it all was accumulating as weight upon our shoulders that we shouldn't have to bear. The stress was producing bouts of anger, and I was having enough of it.

As Jessica was finishing up cooking some pancakes for breakfast, I felt an urgency to go upstairs and pray to get my heart right before the Lord. As I was repenting to Him for how I had been acting, Jesus came in His gentle and loving way and brought a needed calming to my heart.

He told me that He understands what I am going through. He took me out of the woods for a moment to show me from an aerial view all of the things that were coming against us that I wasn't able to see. He revealed that the source of our stress was a demonic attack coming against some new areas of spiritual breakthrough we had been approaching.

Those are not good reasons for behaving the way we did because we are called to a higher standard of maturity than that and carry the necessary equipment to overcome. However, Jesus was bringing great comfort to my heart by releasing His compassion and understanding over me. He understood what we were going through. I didn't feel judged but loved. And once I saw things in the light of how they truly were, Jessica and I were able to gain freedom and peace because of the truth that sets us free.

The point is, if you are ever facing a time of utmost vulnerability before the Lord, don't stop there. Give Him the opportunity to come and speak His compassionate understanding over you about your situation. From there, He will escort you into the deeper place we all long for, a place containing strength and glory.

Arrival Upon Destination

Let me remind you, our whole pursuit in this chapter is the spiritual Sabbath rest of God. We discovered that the journey begins with being true to self, owning up to our weaknesses. Next we learned to accept Jesus Christ's acceptance of us. And now we have arrived at the place where our rest lies—in the ecstasies of God's glory.

Proceeding in Hebrews 4, verse 16 says, *"Therefore let us draw near with confidence to the throne of grace, so that we may receive mercy and find grace to help in time of need."* This is Jesus calling us—the "weak people"—into the very Holy of Holies. We, the seemingly dysfunctional ones, receive the royal V.I.P. invitation to the throne of God. It is a summons for all people who are willing to expose themselves truly to God. We do not have to clean ourselves up before we are worthy to approach His throne. It is at His throne that we receive mercy. It is called the "mercy seat."

Regardless of our condition, He has given us the OK for a face-to-face encounter. In this place, we get more than mercy; we get grace to empower us in the time of need. The Lord doesn't just accept us in our weaknesses; He takes it a step further and imparts strength into us to make us powerful. We end up better than when we started. This is the Sabbath rest.

We get to rest from the work of striving to be something we are not. We get to become the fullness of who God says we are. And we get to enjoy this revitalization process while basking in the glory. A rest in Paradise puts the crystal blue waters of the Bahamas to shame. He has given us complete open access to enter into the ecstatic bliss of His presence and love. Our Sabbath rest is the saturation of *Christ in us* as we enjoy the fruits of our intimate union.

We will talk in the next chapter of the benefits of our access to throne room encounters with God.

14

Hall Passes Through
the Tabernacle

I n the Old Testament, there was a very important man-made structure called the *tabernacle,* which was considered the "house of
God." Although it is impossible to build anything large enough to
contain God, He was gracious enough to rest His manifest presence
inside this tent so His people could be near to Him. Within the port-
able cloth building, there were two holy rooms, which were divided
by a very thick veil. The first was called the holy place and the second
the Holy of Holies. The priests would minister in the first room daily.
In the deeper room sat the mercy seat of God, and His shekinah,
weighty, *kabod* glory rested in there. That was where God sat upon
His throne in manifest form in the midst of His holy people.

The atmosphere was so holy that only the high priest could enter
it one time per year to bring a blood sacrifice. He had to crawl
through a small opening at the bottom of the veil to exit the first
room and enter into the next. Tradition says that the high priest had a
rope tied to his foot and bells around his waist when he entered in.
There would be another priest on the outside of the veil holding the
other end of the rope. The purpose for this was just in case his personal sins did not get properly atoned for and he was struck dead in
the weight of the glory. The other priest would hear the bells jingle
and then stop when he hit the floor; then he would pull the high
priest out so that he would not have to go inside and risk the same
while retrieving him. Hopefully that didn't happen often, if ever.

The temporary Old Covenant tabernacle was a mere shadow of the true eternal tabernacle in Heaven. However, when Jesus died on the cross, the sky went black, a great earthquake shook and split the rocks, and the veil of the earthly temple was torn in two (see Matthew 27:45,51). This was symbolic of what Jesus did in the spirit realm. He has atoned for our sins thoroughly. He has made us worthy to actually minister before God with a clean conscience. First Peter 2:9 says that we have become a royal priesthood. With that veil torn in two, the way has been opened for us all to draw near to the mercy seat in Heaven, the very throne of God. And we don't have to wait until next year to go again.

Hebrews 10:20 says that we can enter into God's holiest place "*by a new and living way which He inaugurated for us through the veil, that is, His flesh.*" In the true tabernacle of Heaven, the veil that separates the two rooms is Jesus' flesh. His body has been broken, making a way to the throne for us. He is the only way that we can come through to get to the Father (see John 14:6). He truly is the open door that provides our way through the veil. Because He is the Lamb of Sacrifice, the Great High Priest, *and* the Open Door, we have thoroughly been given full access to approach the throne of God.

Don't Clean Up to Take a Bath

I used to believe we need to get mercy and cleansing before we dare to approach His holy throne. But it is actually **at His throne** that we get it. "*Let us draw near with confidence to the throne of grace, so that we may receive mercy and find grace to help in time of need*" (Hebrews 4:16). That is why it is also called the mercy seat. We should not approach the throne abashed. You can't approach the throne properly while retaining a guilty conscience. But remember, the moment you turn your heart to the Lord for cleansing is the moment He brings it. This verse says for us to draw near to the throne with confidence. And this is in context with being naked and bare in all of our weakness (as we discussed in the previous chapter). We have to come believing that we are fully accepted already. We can't wait to get mercy; we must go to the throne to get it. Any other belief is one of delusion.

We must believe that we can freely confess our sins and our weaknesses right to God's face in His Holy of Holies. Mercy cancels our debts. Anything we've done wrong is wiped away. It brings us out of the negative and it balances us instantaneously. He has made us worthy to access Him right where He sits.

From Bubbles to Brawns

The goods don't stop at the bathtub of glory though. When I was a little boy, I enjoyed the smelly bubbles, the Noah's Ark accompanied by a squeeze-spray rubber dolphin, and the battery-powered submarine I bathed with in our porcelain, oval ocean. To me, it was a nightly adventure. To Mom, it was a routine challenge to get the backyard scrubbed off my body and the potatoes dug out of my ears. Once she finally convinced me to let her yank me out of the tub when she was done, I realized the fun had only begun. What could be better than the process of getting squeaky clean? Underoos! I instantly got transfigured from a filthy rugrat to Superman. I may not have been able to budge open a sliding glass door on my own; but with my cape on, I could be stopped by nothing.

Along with mercy that wipes away the negative comes the gift of grace that thrusts us high into the positive. It brings us out of the red and into the black, per se. Grace is the power of God, and we become very powerful at the throne. It is in Christ alone that we are strong. We are not powerful on our own. But greater is He who is in us than he who is in the world (see 1 John 4:4). We are powerful because Jesus is in us. God's grace is not just for the forgiveness of sins, nor is it just to give us unmerited favor. It is also a supernatural empowerment from Heaven. Grace is to us what a cape is to Clark Kent. It makes us strong where we are weak.

In 2 Corinthians 12:9, Paul shared Jesus' reply to his plea to be rescued from some problems he was dealing with. "*And He has said to me, 'My grace is sufficient for you, for power is perfected in weakness.' Most gladly, therefore, I will rather boast about my weaknesses, so that the power of Christ may dwell in me.*" Grace is a divine power that dwells within us and perfects us even in our weaknesses. When we accept that we are indeed weak in and of ourselves, then, through faith, Christ will dwell in us in power and grace.

In 2 Corinthians 12:10, Paul goes on to say, *"For when I am weak, then I am strong."* It is not as important that we grow in our own strength as it is that we grow in a dependency upon *God's* strength and power. He doesn't just give us a power to *endure* hardships. It is a power to *rise above* them in dominion. If a person is ever struggling with sin or with problems that he just can't find his way through, this is where the answer lies. Where we were weak, we will become powerful by the empowerment of grace. *"Let the weak say, 'I am strong'"* (Joel 3:10 NKJV).

It is true that God has expectations for us that are far beyond what we are able to accomplish through our own strength. Under the Old Covenant way of thinking, this would be detrimental to spiritual health. It is similar to the Egyptians forcing the Israelites to make bricks without providing the necessary ingredient of straw and still expecting the same results. But God never requires anything from us without giving us the resources we need to succeed. He is a fair and just God. He is looking for godliness and nothing less. But under our current Covenant, He has already provided the power to attain it. It is just up to us to recognize it, receive it, and utilize it.

> *Grace and peace be multiplied to you in the knowledge of God and of Jesus our Lord; seeing that* **His divine power has granted to us everything pertaining to life and godliness**, *through the true knowledge of Him who called us by His own glory and excellence* (2 Peter 1:2-3).

Hebrews 4:16 is one of my most important life verses. As we read earlier, it says, *"Let us draw near with confidence to the throne of grace, so that we may receive mercy and find grace to help in time of need."* It is a three-strand cord that is never to be broken. We receive mercy, we obtain grace, and better than anything else, we get to approach the throne of God boldly. This is not in figurative language. In spirit, we truly get to stand before the throne of God. Regardless of our current circumstance, we are qualified right now to draw near to His throne of grace with confidence. According to this passage in Hebrews 4, the only criteria are faith and a naked and surrendered heart. (See previous chapter regarding nakedness.)

There are many ways that we are able to approach God's throne. Prayer, repentance, worship, or just simply soaking in His goodness are a few. We can actually approach God's throne in daily life activities if we can just believe it. If we approach Him in spirit and truth, which happens by believing, we are literally in posture before the actual throne of God.

Consider this. Next time you go to the Lord in prayer or worship (or whatever your approach), if you could only open the eyes of your heart to see clearly into the spirit realm, you would be induced with shock and awe at the splendor that you would witness. You would literally see God sitting on His throne of radiant glory right before your eyes staring at you face to face! He wants to love on you. You would see Jesus, The Lover of Our Souls, in all of His glory, coming from God's right hand. You would feel His life energy flooding into every fiber of your being.

You would look around and see four living creatures flying in circles around His throne shouting out revelatory hymns that you've never heard. You would realize that you are in company with 24 elders worshiping on their knees, pouring their hearts out in a relentless, passionate love. If you could open your spiritual sinuses, you would smell incense rising up from your prayers; and you would see God breathing in the aroma as it brings Him deep pleasure.

What I am trying to explain is that you, as a Christian, are already granted access into the glory realm. The more you can believe that it is surrounding you even now, the more you will begin to experience it in manifest form. The more you treasure it, the more you encounter it. You and I are already tapped into the essence of this place in spirit. We just need the revelation that such an experience is a present reality in which our spirit already abides. Our minds and hearts need to catch up to the truth of our existence in Christ. We are seated with

Him in heavenly places. What a bummer to miss out on this truth because of inferior beliefs that are commonly produced by doubt, religiosity, and unnecessary shame.

Jesus Stole My Sermon

One time, I was with a ministry team in Madrid, Spain. I was scheduled to preach one evening, and I felt led to share this message on Hebrews 4. Ironically, that afternoon was one of utmost weakness for me. It wasn't in the form of moral failure, but it was in the form of being gripped by fear in my heart.

For some reason, I had subconsciously let the accuser whisper lies into my ear that said I was nothing compared to my teammates. They had been walking in some awesome signs and wonders and getting a lot of attention, and it made me feel small among them. A ridiculous intimidation set in that paralyzed me as I knew I would be preaching right in front of them. What would they think of me if I brought a revelation that differed from theirs?

It was demonically influenced, but I didn't yet recognize it as such. In reality, I had been walking in miracles and spiritual gifts too; but when you listen to the enemy's lies, truth gets clouded over by deception. Even if I had never released a miracle, it should not have even mattered. That is not where my identity comes from. We were out in the city doing tourism all day, and I was getting more and more paranoid the closer we got to the time when we would head back for ministry at the church.

I couldn't take it any longer. I had to break away from my little group to go pray somewhere. I found a park near the bus stop where we were scheduled to meet. I only had about 45 minutes to spare, so I wanted to make the most of it.

At first I started praying in a panic. But the Holy Spirit reminded me that this was no way to get God's attention. So I forced myself to quit striving to overcome the fear by my own strength. Then I started confessing the weakness of anxiety and intimidation that I was dealing with. Once the confession came out, He asked me to receive His peace and love by faith. So by faith, I drew on His peace and love. I actually began to feel it enter in. This mental shift opened me right up to a place where Jesus could actually do something to help. He came and revealed Himself to me in a vision right in that Spanish park.

Then He started reminding me of who I am to Him. He spoke over me how I am a son of God and there is nothing small about me. Rather, because of who He has made me to be, I am powerful. And because the things that I carry for preaching and ministry came from Him, they are powerful. I would be foolish to consider them anything less by comparing them to someone else. That is a good way to devalue something holy. He told me that the only appropriate comparisons that are legal for me to measure myself with are my own past (to show the distance I have come) and Christ (who is already within me).

I felt the bands of wickedness snap right off me; and the weighty spirit of fear perching on my shoulders instantly released its sharp talons and flew away with a tucked tail. All of a sudden, I was feeling free and confident again.

Once we got back to the church, I found a private room where I could go pray and prepare for my sermon. While I was in there with the light off, the glory of the Lord filled the room. It actually got brighter in there. Jesus came and poured His love all over me. Then, instead of giving me the opportunity to use that time for sermon preparation, He hogged up my time by preaching my Hebrews 4 sermon right to me, face to face. I'll admit, that was a better form of sermon preparation than I had planned. It was His message spoken directly into my heart.

He was revealing to me how accepted I am to Him even in my weakness, and how He is the champion who has saved the day and made me strong in Him. Every last bit of the residue of intimidation was broken off of me. His peace and glory washed over me in renewal. My tension turned into tears and my shirt into a dishrag as I bawled my eyes out at the revelation of His extravagant love for me. I found my strength once again.

By the time I finally got the opportunity to preach, I literally felt like I had become intoxicated under the influence of His glorious presence. It made for an interesting sermon. I would probably be embarrassed to watch a video of it. But I wasn't the only one who was being smitten by the manifest love of Jesus in that room. It was happening all over the place.

It was beautiful and awesome how the Lord manifested the virtues of this revelation to us. Later that night, three different people came to tell me about angels they saw coming into the room during the time I was ministering. In the thickness of that atmosphere, I can say I wasn't surprised to hear that. God honored me and His Word. I have since been able to draw from this breakthrough at different times in life to walk in the freedom to be myself, in the fullness of Christ, when faced with the temptation to succumb to fear and intimidation.

This is such a powerful and true message of the easy and open access into the glory realm of God. And we are pressing in for deeper and greater things to come. The only ones who make this experience hard are us—you and me—not God.

15

I May Have Messed Myself

Everybody knows that they have screwed up at times and are still susceptible to make more messes. Most people legitimately hope to not fail or fall but want to live righteously and honorably. We have talked about how important it is to God that we are transparent before Him and own up to our weaknesses. He fully accepts us in our weaknesses, even to the degree of getting down into the gutter with us when we reach those lows. But His intention is not to keep us in the gutter of our weaknesses; it is to lift us up far above them so we can be powerful, free, and victorious. This chapter and the next we will discuss some practical ways of disarming sin and condemnation when they arise so we can protect a lifestyle of freedom.

No Navel-Gazing Allowed

It is crucial when the Lord reveals to us our sins and weaknesses that we own up to them and repent to Him. However, God is not calling on us to become habitual inner fault-seekers. Self-introspection is not a healthy practice for the children of God. My pastor, Bill Johnson, calls this "navel-gazing." This is something the Lord showed me years ago, probably as far back as the time I quit going out to the creek bed altar in self-abasement during my ignorant attempts at repentance.

In 1 Corinthians 4:3-5, Paul explained, "*But to me it is a very small thing that I may be examined by you, or by any human court; in fact, **I do not even examine myself. For I am conscious of nothing against*** *myself, yet I am not by this acquitted; but the one who examines me is the Lord. Therefore do not go on passing judgment before the time, but* **wait until the Lord comes who will both bring to light the things hidden in the darkness and disclose the motives of men's hearts;** *and then each man's praise will come to him from God."* The Greek word for *examine* is *anakrino*, which means "to scrutinize, investigate, interrogate, determine, or judge."

Paul was telling a little secret to his success in living a victorious and confident lifestyle. The secret was that he didn't give any time or attention to self-introspection for weakness (or strength); nor did he come under shame through other people who generously brought it to him. He was clear that he was well aware of having issues, but he also understood that they were no issue until the Lord made them one, and in His time.

God is the judge and we are not; and neither is our neighbor for that matter. Therefore, we are not to even judge ourselves. Rather, we are to maintain a heart that is fully surrendered to God in a posture of complete openness and vulnerability. This should be to the point that if at any moment God addresses an issue, we are quick to respond. It is all about keeping our eyes focused on God, ready to serve Him instantly at any request. The center of our focus should always remain on God and not ourselves.

This is not to say that we should ignore a sin or a problem when we know it is there. Awareness of it qualifies it as exposed and due for demolition. If we are consciously sinning, then we need to stop and repent immediately. To clarify my point, I am specifically suggesting that we shouldn't go on internal witch hunts looking for things that God is not looking for.

I am also not suggesting that Paul had no value for a brother or sister coming to point out a speck in his eye. He is very clear in other passages that we need to look out for one another for protection from the dangers of immorality. He did this often in his letters to the churches. The point is that we shouldn't judge things if we don't see God judging them and inviting us to expose them. Otherwise we'll waste precious time doing what God is not.

(Disclaimer: I am not suggesting we ignore sins that violate other people's wills and put them in harm's way. There is no question that if we see this happening, it is crucial to confront it. Or if it is dangerous, it should be immediately reported to the proper authorities. These kinds of people need help, and sometimes help comes in the form of the law and/or intervention. In this conversation though, I am specifically trying to talk about general issues of the heart that most people deal with, not illegal issues which require protocols.)

All too often, people spend too much of their lives focused on trying to keep themselves clean of things that may not even be issues to God. The more attention we put on our weaknesses and our aptitude for failure, the more depressed we will needlessly make ourselves. If we look for weakness, we are sure to find it. When we do self-introspection, who are we looking at? It is definitely not fixing our eyes on Jesus, the Author and Perfecter of Faith. It is not setting our minds on things above. It is actually a form of self-seeking and an attempt at self-preservation.

Rather than spending so much time trying to hunt down problems in order to avoid them (which sounds like a paradox to me), God would much more prefer that our time be spent abiding in Him. To God, that is where quality time belongs. Intimacy with God is the only sure way to avoid sin and to obtain true inner purity. He is faithful and very good at His job of exposing weaknesses at the right times. Make no mistake about it; He will do it, but in His timing. His method is never to make us feel bad about ourselves or to destroy our confidence. His approach always induces peace and inspires our hearts to love Him more. That is the opposite result from adhering to anyone else as judge. Just remember, God is Judge and we are not. And He rules and reigns in peace.

Dealing with Confrontation

If someone comes to you in judgment, or as a brother who is lovingly trying to point out the speck in your eye, the proper response is to humbly, promptly, and innocently ask God if He agrees. If He confirms it, you have a wonderful invitation to experience refreshing through repentance and some transformation into the image of Christ. If God does not confirm it, you have been presented with an opportunity to: enter into a sentence of condemnation, get offended, or let it roll off your shoulders and confidently carry on your business with a forward stride. This obviously should never be done with bitterness against the brother providing accountability. It should be done, as everything should, *"with all humility and gentleness, with patience, showing tolerance for one another in love, being diligent to preserve the unity of the Spirit in the bond of peace"* (Ephesians 4:2-3).

Truth always inspires confidence in the Lord and never condemnation. What is God saying about your situation? That is where the ultimate authority lies. If your friend (or critic) confronts you on an issue that is clearly stated under the New Covenant scripture, then that is probably your answer for what God is saying. (Unless their revelation of its meaning is amiss.) It is always important to make sure we clearly understand what the person is actually trying to say behind all of the extra emotional words they may bark out. We need to learn to value what they really need from us.

Even if, during the confrontation, their heart may not seem to be love, it is still your responsibility to see if there is any truth in the matter that the Lord may want to deal with. It takes a lot of humility to walk this stuff out well. After assessing the situation before the true Judge and thanking the friend for his merciful concern, your response is then between you and God.

The only exclusion to this would be if they approach you about an issue that involves a hindered relationship with someone. At that point, the ultimate goal is reconciliation, not being right. Humbly owning up to an offense committed is crucial because to God there is nothing that takes precedence over family relationships in the Kingdom. He won't even accept an offering at the altar before we've fixed our side of the problem (see Matthew 5:23-24).

God is the only true Judge for whether or not the action you were confronted about is causing interference in your personal connection between Heaven and Earth. People can try to slap guilt on you in punishment for their offended heart, but it is your choice whether or not you will submit to their lordship. Jesus came to set the captives free, not to bind them up. A friend recently asked one of my pastors, Danny Silk, about how to properly respond to confrontational feedback without letting it turn into self-introspection. He said, "Fear turns you inward, and love turns you outward." He explained that fear is what causes us to get seized up over imperfections. Love has the power to recognize a wrong done and reconcile it without letting the heart get all bound up in guilt and shame.

Any time a Christian confronts another for a wrong done it should always be with the attitude of love. It should be from desire to help the other get positioned for greater blessings. It needs to always come from mercy that longs to see the other person experience a greater flow of God's grace in their life. If that is not the motive behind it, then it will have the ability to misdirect the person into religious bondage and/or manipulation. We cannot do this to other people or allow that entrapment to happen to us from their inferior motives. It is important that we always know that God's heart is to make us *more* free and *more* amazing.

Whenever the time comes when we have to face the reality that we sinned or did someone wrong, we are responsible to clean up our messes. Although we are created in the image of God and have the divine nature, we are still in the process of being transformed into the image of Christ. What this means is that until we have reached that end goal, there will probably be recurrences of falling short along the way. But this is never to be treated as punishable failure in the eyes of God. We cannot allow guilt and condemnation to take hold of our hearts and hold us captive. Always remember that our true nature is not sin, it is the holiness of Christ. God still sees the finished product of perfection in us and we must embrace this as we are being transformed into that reality in our practical life.

Our Judge is one who is all about justice. And justice is all about freedom. In justice, He doesn't aim vengeance at us. "*Therefore there is now **no condemnation for those who are in Christ Jesus**"* (Romans 8:1). On the cross, He already brought vengeance on the enticer and on sin itself—"...*sending His own Son in the likeness of sinful flesh and as an offering for sin, **He condemned sin in the flesh**"* (Romans 8:3).

One definition for *condemn* is "to judge or pronounce unfit for use." Sin has been disarmed, disempowered, and condemned in the flesh. When things get condemned, they get demolished, such as old fallen-apart buildings. Jesus has demolished sin from our nature. Our sentence is redemption and liberty. And until God points a fault out to us as an issue to be dealt with, we get to continue on in liberty and advancement. We can experience liberty before, during, and after the issue is dealt with if we keep ourselves fully surrendered to our Savior.

The Doctor is Here to See You

If you are ever in question if there is sin that God wants to point out, I suggest a time of healthy and proper examination. Invite the Holy Spirit to fill you with His presence and supernatural peace. Cultivate this atmosphere through some worship. In worship, open up your heart wide to Him and permit Him to inspect it. Ask Him to reveal to you if there are any spots in there that do not match up to the Christ within you or that are hindering your heart-connection to God. Ask Him to expose any sins, unbelief, or unhealthy mindsets that He wants to deal with. Take a moment and, in His loving presence, consider if there are any repetitious behaviors you have which are not producing good fruit. It is important that through the leading of the Spirit we discover the source of where these behaviors or poor beliefs are coming from.

Keep in mind to refrain from navel-gazing. In other words, do not search for sin by your own wisdom, but allow the Holy Spirit to reveal things He may see.

This should be done with the same approach David had in Psalm 139. He was well aware of God's amazing love for him. Psalm 139:17 says, "*How precious also are Your thoughts to me, O God! How vast is the sum of them!*" In that context of love, he went on to inquire of Him—"*Search me, O God, and know my heart; try me and know my anxious thoughts; and see if there be any hurtful way in me, and lead me in the everlasting way"* (Psalm 139:23-24). David had a tender heart for the Lord and eagerly wanted to know if there was anything in his heart that was hindering his walk with God. But rather than soul-searching, he asked God to do it in him.

This is no time for condemnation. Remember, God accepts you as you are and wants you to not be afraid to get naked before Him. This is a high honor to Him. Do not try to conjure up old sins of which you have already been forgiven. You will only waste precious time with that because to Him they do not exist. Do not move into self-introspection or you will more than likely get a false diagnosis to the root cause. When God unveils sin, He is laser-point accurate and brings the necessary instruments for surgical healing and restoration.

His approach has nothing to do with punishment; it has to do with freedom. He is a good Father whose intentions are solely to position us to get under His greater blessing. Holy Spirit wants to bring His love sword in and liberate you from the roots of sin; to free you from the lasting effects of that old false nature that for so long has felt like your true nature. His procedures are not always fun during the process, but they are always rewarding. They transform us into the nature of Christ.

If He highlights any area of sin or inferior thinking, ask Him to forgive you. Do not hurry through this. Sometimes it is very important to take some time to let God expose the depth of the sin and to repent in equal measure. It won't be the same depth for everyone or for every situation. Again, do not let shame have room in this. However, it is healthy to let godly sorrow fill that area. It is OK to grieve as you consider the effect your sin has had on God, on others, and on yourself. The deeper you let Him cut into that place, the deeper you will get your healing.

The goal here is not just a clean slate; it is a transformed life. God's mercy is filling you. Celebrate His amazing forgiveness and take joy in it! He never withholds forgiveness and cleansing from us. But we don't just want to get forgiven; we want to tap into that place where we know that we are utterly weak and must have His strength or we will die. It is in the place of vulnerability and weakness that His grace is able to come in and extract the root of sin, heal the wound that gave it the entry point, and empower us to be victorious. This is the chance for Jesus to become manifested in us in new and greater ways.

If the Lord has exposed an area of sin for you to repent of, ask Him to reveal to you where that sin came in. In other words, was there a lie that you believed, a heart wound that still needs healed, a person you need to forgive, or a person you need to repent to, etc.? Usually repeated sinful behaviors have something hidden underneath them that are causing these things to sprout up like weeds. Until that thing is identified, the true problem hasn't been solved.

If He exposes a lie or a wounded place, ask Him to speak His truth into that situation. Ask Him to heal that area and restore wholeness to it. If there is reconciliation to be made, confess out of your mouth before God that you forgive the person, or that you want forgiveness. If it involves that person directly, it is so important to go to them if physically possible and reconcile. (The only out for this is if the person is dead or it is somehow physically impossible to get in touch with them; but even still it is helpful to vocalize your part of reconciliation as if God were sending the message to them. It helps bring closure.)

We shouldn't be content until the issue is annihilated. Of course, we never should do this with our own wisdom or strength. It needs to always be Spirit led or we are back in the same old shackles. Sometimes it just takes time and work as we co-labor with Christ, (especially when our issues are wounding other people). It often may require the help of other trusted people in our lives to partner with us through the process if we can't seem to conquer it on our own. "*Brethren, even if anyone is caught in any trespass, you who are spiritual, restore such a one in a spirit of gentleness; each one looking to yourself, so that you too will not be tempted. Bear one another's burdens, and thereby fulfill the law of Christ*" (Galatians 6:1-2). (We will discuss more about outside help in the next chapter.)

Don't give up. Celebrate incremental successes as you make gains in the right direction. The Lord is faithful to perfect us as we partner with Him. The most important role we play in this process is the renewing of our minds towards truth by the washing of the water with the word (see Ephesians 5:26). Believing the truth in our hearts brings us into freedom and empowers us to say "No!" to the cravings that entice us.

And do not be conformed to this world, but be transformed by the renewing of your mind, so that you may prove what the will of God is, that which is good and acceptable and perfect (Romans 12:2).

Transformation always follows mind renewal. This is what true repentance is.

Do not spend time trying to find sins that God is not going after. The sin-mining days are over. The goal is to maintain a soft heart before the Lord that He is invited to have Lordship over. It is time to celebrate the goodness of God and intimacy with the One who loves you just the way you are.

The Therapeutic Turn-Around

It is impossible to buy favor from God. Grace is not for sale. True repentance is sincerely turning the heart away from things void of God and surrendering them wholly to Him. It is more than just saying "I'm sorry." It is shifting our affections back to the Lover of our souls, receiving His free gift of grace by faith. It is adjusting our mindsets to match His. We cannot work hard enough in paying penance to convince God to forgive us of anything. He has already done it fully.

*When you were dead in your transgressions and the uncircumcision of your flesh, He made you alive (resurrected) together with Him, **having forgiven us all our transgressions**, having canceled out the certificate of debt consisting of decrees against us, which was hostile to us; and He has taken it out of the way, having nailed it to the cross (Colossians 2:13-14).*

Repentance does not require us to enter into a season of grief and sorrow. The only sorrow God wants for us is the kind that leads us into repentance (see 2 Corinthians 7:9-10). But that sorrow can be left at the curb once we have restored our affections back where they belong. God's plan for repentance is to bring us into seasons of happiness. "*Repent therefore and be converted, that your sins may be blotted out, so that **times of refreshing may come from the presence of the Lord**"* (Acts 3:19 NKJV). The result of true repentance is "times of refreshing" in the presence of the Lord, which causes joy.

Nehemiah had the privilege of restoring the city of Jerusalem and its walls back to code after it had been demolished when Israel was taken into captivity many decades prior. However, through this process, there was something much more important being restored—God's beloved people. The reason they had suffered disaster in the first place was because of the sins of the nation. As they were rebuilding the city, the lost book of God's law was discovered in the temple. By this time, the people were hungry for God and eager to learn of His ways.

The entire nation gathered around Ezra the priest to listen to him read God's Word aloud. They were not familiar with the Word because they had been absent from it for a very long time. When it got to the parts that declared certain actions as sin and detestable to God, their hearts were torn in grief because they suddenly realized they had broken many of His laws. In repentance, they were all weeping their guts out.

What followed seemed contradictory to all things religious. Nehemiah responded to their cries by telling them to stop mourning and weeping and begin partying instead. He said, "*Go, eat of the fat, drink of the sweet, and send portions to him who has nothing prepared; for this day is holy to our Lord. **Do not be grieved, for the joy of the LORD is your strength**"* (Nehemiah 8:10). To God, our repentance is a reconnecting with His goodness and is supposed to be a restoration of His joy and peace inside of our heart—not a gloomy time of self-pity. It is through **His joy** that we have the strength to live righteously for Him.

If you aren't experiencing freshness in His presence, you probably haven't experienced complete repentance in the faith. Remember, repentance is simply shifting your mindsets to match His; and His mindset always bring peace. *"The steadfast of mind You will keep in perfect peace, because he trusts in You"* (Isaiah 26:3). If this is not your experience after repentance, you have probably either tried to cleanse yourself from your own sin or still have yet to discover some truths of His grace for you.

The truth is that if you are a child of God, He has already blotted out your sins. For the born-again believer, repentance is not so much about ridding oneself of a tie to sin, but about renewing our mind to the fact that Jesus has already removed sin's grip from our nature. He truly has set us apart. Knowing this brings ease in our ability to simply step away from the loosened grasp of sin, temptation, and destructive habits.

As mentioned before from Hebrews 10:22, the cleansing of sin is a guarantee when we approach the throne of grace. It's the same as the guarantee of my car getting cleansed from gravel dust and bug guts as I drive it into a car wash. The further in I get, the cleaner the car gets. Did you know that the headwaters of the River of Life actually spring forth from the Throne of God? (See Revelation 22:1.) It is as we approach His throne (which is also called the mercy seat) that our bodies are washed in pure water and we are truly made clean. It is no wonder that we find refreshing in the presence of the Lord.

If you still need to experience peace and refreshing in His presence, maybe now is your moment! Take some time to get away from distractions and believe for an encounter with God. As you posture yourself for an experience with Him, do these things:

- If you have sins for which you haven't asked forgiveness, ask and believe He has done it.
- If you have no more sins to confess, understand that He has already cleansed you from all sins in the blood of Jesus (see 1 John 1:7, 9) and it is a done deal.
- Meditate on the reality that you are squeaky clean in His sight (see Ephesians 1:4).
- Believe that He has made you worthy of His goodness.
- Let Him convince your heart that He is thoroughly pleased

with you as His beloved child, and that He truly enjoys your company.

- Meditate on the fact that He is at complete peace in His thoughts toward you (see Ephesians 1:2 and Luke 2:14).
- Believe that He wants to encounter you more than you want Him to (see John 14:21).
- Ask the Holy Spirit to fall on you, and relax while believing that He is doing it right now. Jesus said that all you have to do is thirst and believe that you are drinking the living water, and it will fill you up to the point of spilling over like a river out of you. So drink in faith (see John 7:37-39).
- If you don't already have a method for meditating that comes natural to you, you can try one of my favorites. I like to do what some call "soaking." I will play some soft, worshipful music. (My preference is instrumental for this purpose because lyrics tend to influence my train of thought.) Resting comfortably, either in a reclining chair or by lying on my back on the floor, I engage with the music while letting the Holy Spirit settle upon me. I exercise yielding my attention to whatever Holy Spirit wants to express from the Scripture, a thought, or a feeling. Then, remaining in a relaxed state, I will ponder on this until it affects my spirit, soul, and body in a needed way.
- Enjoy!

16

I Definitely Messed Myself, Now What?

S o what if God has searched my heart and found that there are some hurtful ways within me? What if He has highlighted an area in my life where recurring sins and/or bad habits keep showing up? What if I keep "messing myself" and can't seem to stop? If so, God obviously is ready to do some repair work in a broken place in the heart so that area can be brought into His loving blessings once again. The victory belongs to the Lord; but He needs our partnership in order to make it manifest in our lives. There are some practical things we can do to co-labor with Christ in order to gain new measures of strength and freedom. Applying these keys will help bring an end to our tendency for falling into the sins that so easily entangle us.

Key #1: Take Every Belief Captive

We are all capable of sinning. But when we give our lives to Christ, sin is no longer part of our nature. The old, sinful body was crucified with Christ and we have been raised with Him as new creations. This means that whatever weaknesses we thought were part of who we are, actually are not part of us. Within us is the Spirit of Holiness. If I sin, I am choosing to partner with a force that is external to my spirit-man. God told Cain, "*If you do not do well, sin is crouching at the door; and its desire is for you, but you must master it*" (Genesis 4:7). It is on the exterior looking for a way to get inside.

"But each one is tempted when he is drawn away by his own desires and enticed. Then, when desire has conceived, it gives birth to sin; and sin, when it is full-grown, brings forth death" (James 1:14-15 NKJV). In other words, when we choose to yield to temptation through enticement, our hearts become impregnated with sin and give birth to sinful behaviors. Pregnancy only happens by allowing an external source to enter in and impart its virtue. Sin does not spring forth from our nature; it comes from making the decision to bring something in that wasn't present before. And as soon as we confess it and get cleansed in the blood of Jesus, it is no longer present. Sin is a **foreign** substance that cannot be attributed to who you are.

Sin does not have the power to change your identity from who God has declared you to be. You are still a child of the Most High God. What sin can do, unfortunately, is separate your current state of being from your true identity and bring you into a state of delusion.

The prodigal son never stopped being a son who was welcome in his father's home. But his sin separated his experience from his identity and brought him into a false reality of who he thought he was. In delusion, he thought he was a low-life heathen separated from his father and unworthy in his home. In his attempt to come back and earn the right to be on his father's property as an entry-level servant through self-humiliation and works, he was stunned to see his father running to him bringing full acceptance and full restoration to the royalty he once knew.

In order to avoid living lives that are inferior to the ones God has ordained for us, it is very important that we live according to the truth. The devil, the world, and religion will do everything they can to convince us that our sins are a part of who we are. But Romans 6:11 says to *"reckon yourselves to be dead indeed to sin, but alive to God in Christ Jesus our Lord"* (NKJV). There is a conflict of voices, and we have to choose which one to believe and anchor ourselves to it. Wavering in our beliefs will dip us in and out of delusion and compromise the freedom to experience our true identities.

The more we identify with a sin or a weakness as our own, the more we empower its influence and succumb to its strength. But the more we identify with the truth that we are partakers of a divine nature which doesn't contain corruption (see 2 Peter 1:4), the more we empower ourselves with holiness and the virtue to live in freedom.

We all need to proactively take dominion over our belief systems. It should be a lifestyle habit to continually seek God for an increasing revelation of truth from a subjective position, giving Him the opportunity to show us that we may at times need an upgrade in our ideas and interpretations. If what we believe to be truth does not line up with what God calls truth, something is eventually going to budge…and I guarantee it is not going to be God. If we truly want to live our lives devoted to Him, we must be okay with recognizing lies we tend to believe and choose to annihilate them with truth.

The enemy has waged a full-on war with our beliefs. If he can get us to consider his lies, he has us bound. But if we can believe truth, we will live freely. Truth wins every time.

*For the weapons of our warfare are not of the flesh, but divinely powerful for the destruction of fortresses. We are **destroying speculations** and every lofty thing raised up against **the knowledge of God**, and **we are taking every thought captive** to the obedience of Christ (2 Corinthians 10:4-5).*

It isn't just with our own strength that we fight. God has given us divinely empowered weapons to use in the warfare the enemy brings against us. It isn't a battle with the flesh. It is a battle with the mind. The devil tries to deceive us into believing lofty lies and speculations that oppose the knowledge of God. The way we win is by taking every thought captive and bringing them into obedience with Christ. In other words, disciplining our thought lives to make them line up with the mind of Christ. As I often repeat, it is all about the renewing of the mind. We don't conquer the devil by wrestling him to the ground. We conquer him by taking our own thoughts captive, by setting our minds on things above despite all the things of this Earth that try to distract us.

If you need to conquer a sin that "so easily entangles" you, take the thoughts of temptation captive and bring them into the obedience of

Christ. If you have sinful habits that feel like they are just a part of who you are and cannot be changed, destroy the speculation that has risen against the knowledge of God. He says your nature is holy and righteous. If you feel like you are weak, then call yourself strong (see Joel 3:10). The best first step to conquering sin and weakness is to cultivate a new habit of confessing the truths of God over yourself, like this:

"I am more than a conquerer through Him who loves me." (Romans 8:37)

"I am holy and blameless in His sight." (Ephesians 1:4)

"Greater is He who is in me than he who is in the world." (1 John 4:4)

"I am full of the Holy Spirit and bear good fruit." (Galatians 5:16, 22-25)

"I am always triumphant because God leads me." (2 Corinthians 2:14)

"Faith comes from hearing, and hearing by the word of Christ" (Romans 10:17). The more we declare God's truth over ourselves, the more faith will rise up in our hearts to actually believe the words about ourselves and Christ within us. The word of God is like a seed, and the more we speak it and ponder it, the more it takes root and grows and bears good fruit. The more it becomes a part of who we are, the more we begin manifesting it and finding that we are actually able to live it. That is how we take every belief captive and bring it into the obedience of Christ. This is where victory begins: knowing the truth.

Key #2: Build Safeguard Structures

There is a famous quote from a seemingly anonymous author that says, *"Insanity is doing the same thing over and over again and expecting different results."* I am not one to go around diagnosing people with insanity, but I will say that it would be pretty crazy to think one can try to overcome their problems by sheer willpower without changing the structures that surround the problem. The best way we can exercise will-power is by choosing to build wise structures around ourselves that set us up for success. Setting up boundaries and exercising self-discipline to adhere to them is a vital key to gaining needed victories.

I highly doubt that the Tree of Life was planted in the Garden of Eden next to the Tree of the Knowledge of Good and Evil. If Adam and Eve found themselves struggling with the enticements of the forbidden fruit, they could have come up with a purity plan to veer out of range. There are things we need to do to avoid evil at all costs. It is not that being near that tree was bad. But if they stepped within a range where enticement could overpower their vulnerability, they were doing themselves a disfavor. It is very important that we understand our weaknesses, not for the sake of self-abasement, but for the sake of setting up wise boundaries. If a person knows his weaknesses, he can come up with a plan to steer clear of the things or the people that may entice him.

In Proverbs 5, Wisdom is instructing its sons in how to avoid the snares of the adulteress. In Proverbs 5:7-9 Wisdom says, *"Now then, my sons, listen to me and do not depart from the words of my mouth. Keep your way far from her and do not go near the door of her house, or you will give your vigor to others and your years to the cruel one."* The counsel is simple: cling to the wise words of God and keep a healthy distance from the woman who may entice, even avoiding her house altogether.

This is not to say that it is wrong in and of itself to interact with a woman of this nature. I have friends who have a very strong calling to reach out to prostitutes and show them the genuine, non-sexual love of Christ; and Jesus is melting broken women's love-deprived hearts in healthy ways they have needed for years. But if a person is not yet triumphant with freedom in that area of his heart, he is wise to avoid it at all costs to save his vigor and preserve his years.

Regardless of whether the sin pattern has anything to do with lust or any other form of weakness, the issue is the same. Steer clear from environments that may have once enticed you until you are convinced beyond the shadow of a doubt that you have been made a new creation and that this old craving has completely passed away. We need to do whatever it takes to keep ourselves unstained from sin.

The Sacrifice of Boundaries

We all need to get radical about breaking existing harmful patterns. If someone wants to stop getting bitten by a snake, he should cut off its head. If we want to live lives filled with the glorious presence of Christ in every way possible, it may be time to rid ourselves of all things crowding out the space that He wants to occupy, even if it cramps our style for awhile.

For example, if you find yourself susceptible to lust and pornography, maybe it is a good plan to cancel your cable or satellite service, or to cut off your internet and relearn how our pioneer parents once lived without it. Maybe empowering your wife (or someone else if you're not married) to be the only one with the code to get on is needed. What would you do if your Netflix account stirs an unhealthy curiosity when you browse through the blockbuster movies and your eyes pass over a lot of raunch? Or perhaps you are in an unhealthy relationship outside of covenant that continually winds up in sexual sin and you cannot stop. Whatever the problem is, is it worth holding onto for momentary pleasures at the expense of purity and wholeness? It might be time to take the bold step of ending the relationship. We need to get radical with purity, holiness, and wholeness.

I am not just speaking of sinful actions. I am addressing anything that can bring us into bondage and cause us to miss the blessed fruits of His loving presence. Some people have recurrences in life where they find themselves continually shrinking back into fear, depression, or other types of weaknesses that oppose the peace and joy of God in their lives. Oftentimes these ongoing situations are self-induced by embracing soul-ties to relationships, commitments, items, or environments that serve as a memorial or even a source for breeding darkness. For most people in these situations, a drastic change is crucial for victory.

This is by no means an attempt to induce legalism. It is not about rules. It's about safeguards appropriate to the need. How far are you willing to go to demonstrate to God that He holds more value to you than anything else? Find your sacrificial boundaries that will provide safety and ensure you relief from unnecessary enticements. Doing so gives God something to work with in the deeper realms of your heart and mind while you are in a state of non-distraction.

Many years ago as a single man, the practical steps required to finally conquer my old, cyclical porn habit began by unplugging my Internet (back when we used to have cords) and making it hard to get on there without having to consciously go out of my way to do it. In addition, I didn't permit myself to get on the Internet after 9 p.m. or when I was getting tired because I was aware that the later it got, the easier I fell.

I knew that was the level of safety that I needed at the time. It kept me more intentional about what I was doing so I wouldn't slip into those unpredictable moments of vulnerability that were rarely premeditated. Between that, avoiding movie channels, and accountability with close friends and leaders, I was more easily postured to find my soon-coming breakthrough into an enduring freedom I had needed for quite some time. If that level of protection hadn't cut it, I would have needed to upgrade my level of personal security. Thankfully, it cut it for me.

The boundaries themselves were not my victory. The true victory came in my personal relationship with Jesus. He was ministering to my heart and pumping strength into me. I had friends and a mentor walking with me and encouraging me with grace and truth. A mentor led me through an inner healing program called *Freedom in Christ* that helped me gain freedom and strength. The external boundaries I set up for myself provided a safe atmosphere for God to work healing into my heart with less distraction.

It's All About the Heart

Jesus once met with a rich, young ruler who was inquiring about how to live a more abundant life. The young man asked, "*Teacher, what good thing shall I do that I may obtain eternal life?*" Jesus answered, "*If you wish to enter into life, keep the commandments.*" The man asked which ones He was referring to. Jesus listed a few of the top 10. The ruler replied, "*All these things I have kept; what am I still lacking?*" It is interesting that this guy lived a religious lifestyle according to good works, but somehow he knew something was missing on the inside. His personal righteousness would no longer cut it now that he stood in the presence of the Holy One. So Jesus answered, "*If you wish to be complete, go and sell your possessions and give to the poor, and you will have treasure in heaven; and come, follow Me*" (Matthew 19:16-21).

The young ruler probably choked on that one. Up until that final commandment, he was able to check off each personal accomplishment in the "beyond expectations" category of Jesus' registry of good deeds. Yet somehow he still wasn't experiencing the abundant life. Jesus isn't nearly as interested in how well we are obeying the rules as He is in our personal freedom. He was able to see beyond the orderly exterior of this man's religious lifestyle and identify an area of his life that was binding him up internally. It was that area which He chose to address, requesting a radical decision from the man.

God has not made it a rule that every Christian needs to go and sell their possessions for the poor in order to follow Him and be made complete. The reason Jesus gave this directive to the rich, young ruler was because he embraced the love of money, which is a root of all kinds of evil (see 1 Timothy 6:10). His heart was exposed— he loved riches more than God. This hidden sin was hindering his ability to receive the life source of God's presence, and Jesus wanted him free. He was trying to set this man up for success.

Eternal life would not have come from ridding himself of riches; it would have come from following Jesus wholeheartedly. Jesus' goal was not to remove money from this man; it was to remove this man from the environment that so easily ensnared him so he could follow Jesus without the unnecessary distraction. He was trying to lead him into a boundary that would safeguard his heart so he could experience the connection with God that he was lacking (see Matthew 19:16-24.)

The Lord earnestly desires freedom for us so we can live in the fullness of His abundant life. When there are areas of weakness to sin, we need to be aware of how the Lord wants us to take action with it. He strongly urges us to do what it takes to remove ourselves from the sins and environments that so easily pull us down. It takes some measure of sacrifice in order to do this. "... *Let us also lay aside every encumbrance* (hindrance) *and the sin which so easily entangles us, and let us run with endurance the race that is set before us, fixing our eyes on Jesus, the author and perfecter of faith...*" (Hebrews 12:1-2). Removing ourselves from the things that bind us up internally sets us up for what really matters most—the ability to lock eyes with Jesus and behold His glorious face.

Each person's situation is different, some more extreme than others, but the answer always requires sacrifice. Distance from the enticers of weakness is a crucial step away from disappointment and into success. What boundaries do you need to use to safeguard yourself from the pulls you may experience in your unique area(s) of weakness?

Key #3: Choose Your Bandwagon

Another thing a person can do to help avoid temptations and take dominion over weaknesses is to evaluate the crowds he is running with and change them if necessary. There is no question that who we are hanging out with is who we are becoming more like. A lot of times, even spouses end up looking like sister and brother. It's just a fact of nature, a law of influence. Unfortunately, when we knit ourselves to people of the worldly nature, we will in time become conformed more to that same way of life.

That is why Paul said, "*Do not be unequally yoked* (connected) *together with unbelievers. For what fellowship has righteousness with lawlessness? And what communion has light with darkness?*" (2 Corinthians 6:14 NKJV). This verse is referring more to a soul-tie or camaraderie than to a looser association which we all need to maintain if we are to be effective salt and light in the world. Paul also taught, "*Do not be deceived: 'Bad company corrupts good morals'*" (1 Corinthians 15:33). If the people we are hanging out with are living in the same sins or are under the same lies that we are trying to overcome, we don't need Sigmund Freud to tell us that they are doing us more damage than good. Do you have any unhealthy influences in your life?

It is very important to choose wisely who will get our time and gain access to influence our open and vulnerable hearts. It is these people who will affect the molding of our personalities and the outcome of our lifestyles. Whatever fruits they are producing are the same kinds of seeds that they are planting in our hearts and minds. Is that the outcome you desire for your future? It's an important question to ask yourself as you consider who should be your close peers.

Proverbs 13:20 says it clearly: "*He who walks with wise men will be wise, but the companion of fools will suffer harm.*" Therefore, it is very important that we find the people who are heading in the same direction that we are trying to go so we can "*consider how to stimulate one another to love and good deeds*" (Hebrews 10:24). If we can find people who are strong in areas where we are not, we can gain strength from their victories in ways that we lack on our own. (This can only happen through honoring them, or we will become the fool who will cause them to suffer harm.) It is easier to be a winner when you are working with a winning team.

Speaking of partnership, as I have mentioned before, one of the most important first steps to our victory is confession (see 1 John 1:7-9). It is very helpful when we have recurring weaknesses, struggles, temptations, or sins that we find someone godly who we can really trust and to whom we can open up our hearts transparently with no holds barred. Otherwise, isolation is the best way to remain defeated. God designed us to need one another in order to be strong.

An even better option is to take accountability to the level where we can confess issues we sense are coming upon us **before** we have a chance to succumb to them. This can help avoid a fallout altogether. Transparency and vulnerability are necessities in the Kingdom of God. Thus we need to make sure we are surrounding ourselves with people who can help us be strong so we can win. The best kind are those who have a heart to see you thrive, not those who enjoy the opportunity for a power trip. With whom is God leading you to cultivate this kind of relationship?

Can I take it even a step further? The ultimate kind of friendship is one in which you can genuinely invite your trusted friend into a freedom to safely point out to you areas that he sees need improvement in you which may have gone unnoticed by you. We call those areas "blind spots," and this approach is what we call "feedback." What a relationship of trust and transparency this could be! Proverbs 27 has a few words of wisdom on this kind of relationship.

> Better is open rebuke than love that is concealed....Faithful are the wounds of a friend, but deceitful are the kisses of an enemy....Oil and perfume make the heart glad, so a man's counsel is sweet to his friend....Iron sharpens iron, so one man sharpens another (Proverbs 27:5-6,9,17).

There must be openness and freedom to expose ourselves in the light. "If we walk in the Light as He Himself is in the Light, we have fellowship with one another, and the blood of Jesus His Son cleanses us from all sin" (1 John 1:7). Darkness is where mold, bacteria, germs, and all kinds of evil things grow and crawl. The best solution is to open up the windows and shades to let the sunlight and fresh air in. Not only is it liberating and refreshing to get our hidden junk out in the open, it also invites the strength of someone else to lend a hand in bringing additional "overcoming power." "Confess your sins to one *another, and pray for one another so that you may be healed. The effective prayer of a righteous man can accomplish much*" (James 5:16).

Key #4: Get Inner Healing

The goal of this chapter is not to try to create an exhaustive "To-Do List for Conquering Sin." It is strictly just a few practical common sense steps to take. Most of them deal with managing the fruit of the sin but do not necessarily deal with the root problem on their own. The point of these structures is not to give the illusion that, if they get mastered, then everything is peaches and cream. If that were the case, we can scrap the gift of grace and just live by law.

Conquering these behaviors does not resolve the deeper issues of the heart. If all we deal with are the weeds of a certain sin but don't hit the root issue, it will find other places to pop up unnoticed while we are guarding that one crack in the pavement. As we are getting applause for conquering an apparent weakness, the real problem still remains. Usually outward sins are just symptoms of a deeper undetected problem that, a lot of times, comes from an unhealed wound or a lie that is yet to be exposed. If we never deal with the place of brokenness that pushes us to such limits in the first place, there is going to be a new problem that will come up somewhere else in just a matter of time.

However, as I hope it has resounded through this entire message, the big deal with God is not about our sin or about how hard we try to overcome it. It is about the heart and about it being postured honestly and wholly before the Lord so it can enjoy the fullness of God. These practical actions are very necessary, but also are simply tools we can use to remove unnecessary distractions for a season. They help to sustain us while we are in process of the more important matter, which is the renewing of the mind and healing of the heart. If our mindsets don't change to recognize how great God is in us and how great we are in Him, we can only take vacations from sin.

These structures are made to create a sterile environment to give the Master Surgeon a safe, clean place to perform the more needed cardiac surgery. It is the matters of the heart and what we believe about God and ourselves that will truly empower us to overcome the grip of sin.

God is more than capable to transform us into new and much-improved people. *"Therefore if anyone is in Christ, he is a new creature; the old things passed away; behold, new things have come"* (2 Corinthians 5:17). In light of this scripture, I find it difficult to endorse the motto that says, "Once an alcoholic, always an alcoholic" or "Once a porn addict, always a porn addict." It is true that we need to be aware of our weaknesses in order to avoid pitfalls; but we also need to declare over ourselves the superior truth that we are new creatures and the old things have passed away.

I know this motto is true for the world's system. Heightened safety precautions are needed for people who are still discovering the victory of their true identity. Before a person understands and lives in their freedom in Christ, these programs use such tools as safeguards to protect the afflicted from their vices, similar to what I was saying earlier. But God is in the business of full-on redemptive makeovers, and He can truly transform us into very new creatures, making old lifestyles pass away.

*"Therefore we do not lose heart, but though our outer man is decaying, yet **our inner man is being renewed day by day**"* (2 Corinthians 4:16). It is a daily renewal, and He is continually making us more like Christ and less like the world. A son and daughter of the Most High God can rise to a place above the confession of being a "lifelong addict." God says you are a new creation and that old junk has passed away. It's time for an upgrade in the confessions of a lot of people.

(Disclaimer: This is in no way to suggest that a former alcoholic or addict should discontinue participating in their meetings and maintaining healthy accountability. It is simply an invitation to begin prophesying over ourselves the fullness of Christ's nature in spite of our previous downfalls.)

Conquering Through Love

No matter what we believe in the moment of weakness, there is always a higher truth to which we need to cling. *"For whatever is born of God overcomes the world; and this is the victory that has overcome the world—our faith"* (1 John 5:4). Jesus said, *"If you have faith the size of a mustard seed, you will say to this mountain, 'Move from here to there,' and it will move; and nothing will be impossible to you"* (Matthew 17:20). *"You are from God, little children, and have overcome them; because greater is He who is in you than he who is in the world"* (1 John 4:4).

We carry a power that is stronger than the power of any weakness, sin, or addiction. Through confession of sins, renewal of mind, safeguard boundaries, healthy community, declarations of truth, and inner healing by the Holy Spirit, we can overcome the world. We are more powerful than we know through Christ. We have what it takes to apply truth and live the lifestyle necessary to walk in bold victory.

The greatest key to our victory is not so much in the strength of our willpower or our faith, but it is in the knowledge of the unfailing, extravagant love that Jesus Christ has for us. *"But in all these things we overwhelmingly conquer through Him who loved us"* (Romans 8:37). We overwhelmingly conquer through Jesus and the knowledge of His Agape love for us. It is in the revelation of His unending love for us that we become empowered. The power we walk in is in direct proportion to our knowledge of His love. We can take dominion over our own personal issues through the knowledge of the love of Jesus Christ.

17

More than Conquerors

Yet in all these things we are more than conquerors through Him who loved us (Romans 8:37 NKJV).

If we want to be conquerors, we need to believe in ourselves. We must believe that we are able, through the power of Christ, to conquer anything that opposes us. If we want to be more than conquerors, we need to believe in the radical love that Christ has for us. We need to understand His limitless, unconditional love. Knowing this gracious free gift of love empowers us to live victorious lives beyond what we could do on our own.

Jesus died on the cross to set you free. He didn't set you free so you could become a better Christian. He didn't make you free so you will build a better ministry with which to serve Him. He didn't even do it to bring more glory to His name. *"It was for freedom that Christ set us free"* (Galatians 5:1). His love is so selflessly, generously for your own benefit. All He ever wanted for you was to see you enjoy your freedom with Him.

For some time now, I have been feasting on a passage from Romans that has been providing a lot of nutrients to my soul. I think a regular dose of this truth in the diet will make a heart healthy. Plus, it has a lot of fiber that will help pass the junk through that isn't intended to stick around, things like religiosity and performance mentality. The passage is:

But now apart from the Law the righteousness of God has been manifested (revealed), *being witnessed by the Law and the*

*Prophets, even the righteousness of God through faith in Jesus Christ **for all those who believe**...* (Romans 3:21-22).

Did you catch what this is saying? There is no way anybody can compete with God's righteousness because it is infinite in measure. However, the righteousness of God has been gifted to all who believe. It has come to us through faith in Jesus Christ. In other words, when God looks at you and me, the righteousness He sees in us is not our own. It is His righteousness, and He has given it to us for free. What is righteousness? It is "the state of being holy, innocent, just, and right; to be in right standing, as if to have never sinned." In Christ, your righteousness is no longer as filthy rags. **Your righteousness is equal to God's because it is God's.**

This is better news than we could ever imagine because it means that we never have to wonder if God is unimpressed with us. We never have to feel like we are second rate in His eyes. You are the apple of His eye, the object of His affection. Your latest failure didn't disqualify you because it wasn't your success that qualified you in the first place. It was your belief in Christ. You aren't sitting in economy class any longer. You are now in first class with God, and He has nothing more important to do than visit with you. You are in His inner circle and He adores you. He doesn't like the other people better. He really enjoys you. You are just as worthy of the heart and attention of God as Jesus Christ is.

Understanding that we are loved, fully accepted, and adored by God creates a true sense of freedom. We no longer have to fear failure or walk carefully on eggshells so as to not screw up. As a matter of fact, we don't have time for that kind of stuff any longer. We need to recognize the freedom that we already have in Christ and release ourselves to be free. We need to believe that we are champions and are empowered by His grace to be thriving children of God who are making a difference in this broken world. Champions don't live their lives looking over their shoulders in fear that they might stumble any moment. They are focused on what they can do to conquer any obstacle or opposition ahead of them. They are others-focused more than self-focused.

We must take a look at the bigger picture if we want to accomplish greater things. Our starting point is freedom and righteousness in God's eyes. Our significance has greater potential than our current experience. If we can see this, we can look forward and march onward.

It is God's desire that we rise above our own weaknesses and recognize this life really isn't about us. Our lives have a greater purpose than just trying to overcome our own issues. There is a world full of nations that are waiting to be delivered, discipled, and transformed by the Kingdom. We are surrounded by people daily who are empty and desperate to be filled with something good that will last, and we carry what they need. We all have a significant role to play in God's greater plan, and He actually trusts us to fulfill our destinies. Why wouldn't He? He already thinks you are the greatest thing He's created. He is not waiting for us to become perfect in our own eyes before we step out and start bringing Heaven to Earth. What He is waiting for is to *see* us step out and bring Heaven to Earth.

By the grace that we freely receive through faith, we become empowered to dominate our weaknesses. We are powerful to overcome and make gains in Kingdom expansion. We have to get over ourselves and seize our roles in the bigger picture. It is critical that we get to a place where we actually believe that we are overcomers in the things that used to make us buckle. Otherwise, we are belittling the power of Christ that is at work within us, and we will never make a dent in our amazing potential. Looking at the grand picture and choosing to become part of something bigger than ourselves makes it easier to get over ourselves.

Rise Above the Circumstance

When I was 25 years old, I moved from my hometown of Greenfield, Indiana to Nashville, Tennessee. There were multiple reasons for this, but the main one was that I felt I needed to learn how to grow up into a more mature adult without relying on my parents as a backup plan. Another reason was that I felt I needed a change of environment to expand my friendship base and to grow in my ministry skills.

It was a needed move and a challenging one. I faced many different obstacles over the next several months, which seemingly wanted to beat me out of the ring. But God knew that I had to face some hardships in order to actually grow a spine into my back and "take the bull by the horns," as my dad used to exhort me. It didn't take me long to learn what responsibility looked like when I no longer had others to pick up my slack. In the process of pain, I was stumped and unsure of how to climb over some obstacles and get victory without retreating to my old patterns. I was facing many new challenges such as finances, landing a job, finding housing and such, all at once. I felt hopeless, as I didn't have much experience in taking care of myself, and I didn't have a great track record with jobs with which to build a stellar résumé.

It was in those moments of feeling weak and helpless that God showed up and spoke. He said with authority, "It's time to rise above the circumstances!" Although I felt intimidated by responsibilities that were greater than I was familiar with, He assured me that I was more than capable to conquer them. At the time, those were huge mountains set before me. But things were put into proper perspective when He went on to say, "You are greater than these small issues." I would never want to belittle somebody's problems and call them insignificant; however, what we think to be giant boulders are actually granules to Christ. If we magnify He who is within us, we will realize He is greater than anything in the world, giving us the power to disarm and conquer the things that once overpowered us. Those things become small compared to the God within.

Through His affirmations, I was filled with the confidence of the Holy Spirit. Somehow His words inspired courage in me to stand tall, stick my chest out, square my shoulders, and face my mountains with an authority that made them shrink into molehills.

My enemy, who once intimidated me with harassing taunts, deflated into a little weakling, and I jack-slapped it upside the head and took the title back. I was able to rise above the circumstance with a sober mind, believing again that God would meet me in my need. And He did. And everything worked out just fine.

Never again did I have an excuse to allow such circumstances to intimidate me. Ever since, when giant-sized issues arise that must be conquered, the Lord reminds me to "rise above the circumstances," and that I am "greater than these small issues." God has always helped me get through every Goliath-situation I have ever faced. He has blessed me every time I decided to run courageously towards my giants, with a measly rock and a sling in hand, knowing who was backing me up. My Papa loves me, and He's got me covered.

Truth makes the giants in the land become grasshoppers in my sight. I have learned that when I feel intimidation as I am pursuing a forward advance in life, the feeling often is simply my spirit discerning the fear that those supposed "giants" are emitting because they know they are about to get squashed. It is nice to receive God's perspective on our problems because everything suddenly becomes small compared to Him. It's much better than the alternative perspective.

Glamour Giants in the Workplace

A few years later, after I married my beautiful wife, Jessica, I had a new circumstance to deal with in the workplace. As any man should, I have a strong conviction that I am to keep my heart pure and single for the Lord and for my wife. I am a strong believer in the wisdom of Solomon that says, "*Watch over your heart with all diligence, for from it flow the springs of life*" (Proverbs 4:23). This means to guard your heart in order to protect its fountain that is flowing with rivers of living water. It is important that we keep watch over our hearts to not allow them to get infected by the filthy fingers of anything unholy, nor to allow access to unnecessary temptations. We don't want to let anything dirty come and taint the pure and holy things of God.

However, in diligence to keep my heart guarded, I somehow became obsessive. I actually got to the place where I was ignorantly living in paranoia that my heart would fail me in the moment I might relax my vigilance. The fear of failing became a stronghold to me.

In the workplace, I had developed what I considered a safeguard to protect me from any opportunity to stumble. My method of safety was to make every attempt possible to avoid all extremely attractive women in order to avoid lusting. This was not even an issue that I had still been struggling with or internally desiring. I was (and still am) very happy with Jessica and nobody else could replace that. But I had some kind of fear that if I thought someone was attractive, the devil might find a loophole somewhere with which he could snare me. So I went the extra distance to guard my heart even from potential future problems that didn't currently exist. The problem is that any time we are driven by fear to be holy, it is no longer true holiness.

There was one lady in particular who was probably the prettiest woman in the entire three-story building, and she worked near my area. If I had to go to the restroom and saw she was coming my way, I would nervously turn the other direction acting like I had remembered something I had to do. I would go the long way around to get there if necessary. All of that was just so I wouldn't have to interact with her. Continuously, I was guarding my heart as to not even give it a moment's chance to stumble.

I thought this was a noble cause... up until the Lord called me out on it. I would typically spend my break times going on short prayer walks or reading my Bible. It was fairly common that the topics of prayer revolved around needing God's help to overcome personal weaknesses. In other words, I did a lot of navel-gazing. If strength comes by the hours you plead with God for more help to overcome weakness, by that time I should have felt like Conan the Barbarian. But my strength never really seemed to surpass that of Conan O'Brien.

While I was pacing back and forth on that sidewalk near the road, God spoke into my heart, "How long do you plan on struggling under the fear of failing?" This caught me off guard. He continued, "You can continue battling relentlessly to guard the purity of your heart if you wish. Or you can rise above the problem knowing that you are already far more powerful than this petty issue."

God reminded me that I am seated in the heavenly places in Christ, and all other things of this world are beneath my feet as they are beneath His. He told me that I can continue striving for perfection in this area, or I can rest in Him and in who I am in Him. He explained that I have permission to trust that my heart is already pure, and that He is powerful enough to help me keep it pure with ease as I remain in partnership with Him.

He went on to tell me about this particular woman whose external beauty intimidated me. He said that, believe it or not, she actually had an empty and sad heart hidden in there that He wanted to heal. He gently rebuked me for always setting so much of my attention on me and my weakness that I had become blinded to the needs of the hurting people around me. How many other hurting people had gone unseen because I was navel-gazing? I held their answers but not the awareness of their need.

He reminded me that spiritual people look at others on the inside, not the outside. I should have been looking at her after the spirit, not the flesh. I should have believed I could extend Christ's love to her instead of believing I was prone to stumble in lust. I was on the journey of learning that my old man that used to be prone to sin had already been crucified, and it is no longer I who live but Christ who lives within me (see Galatians 2:20). I was powerful because I was a new creation carrying the DNA of Christ, united with Him in fullness of spirit. In Christ, I was prone to fruitfulness, strength, and success.

Once again, God's words imparted courage to my heart, and I rose up feeling powerful. I already had victory; I didn't have to win it. We do not fight *for* victory, we fight *from* victory. In Christ we are on the offense, not the defense. I was able to relax and feel safe, and this liberated me. I quickly discovered that I could now walk in confidence and be myself around anybody. I was no longer seized up in a spiritual straitjacket. Now that I found the freedom that God had already given me, He was able to work through me in a way He had been wanting to for some time.

The very first time that I was able to talk to this lady with internal peace was ironically the time that she felt inspired to share with me some burdens that she had been carrying. They had been weighing her down. She confirmed what the Lord had revealed to me about being empty-hearted and sad. You would never see this on the outside of her Cover Girl smile; but God saw her heart.

I was full of the Holy Spirit and anointed to share the gospel of God's love with her. She was deeply touched, and I was still free from the fear of lust. She let me pray for her to be touched by God's goodness, and His peace settled upon her. All the tension, stress, and anxiety that had become part of her lifestyle vanished. Several days later, she thanked me for praying for her because she was still feeling much better. I was encouraged to see that I had imparted into her the peace I now carried. My breakthrough was passed on to her.

It was amazing to learn that my personal issues were actually hindering me from recognizing that people around me were hungry for an encounter that I could deliver. God showed me that I would never get anywhere in my calling if all I was focused on was my own heart's issues. He needs us to be outward-focused, not stuck being inward-focused. (Obviously there are times when we have to deal with the matters of the heart, but we can't remain there.) When we love God first, and then love our neighbors as ourselves, we will be empowered to conquer more than Conan the Barbarian ever could. When we understand the victory that is already ours, we are able to take dominion over any weakness or mountain that stands in our way.

God led me to take this step of risk because He knew my heart wasn't in the same place that it had been years before when I struggled with lust. If He had seen that I was still weak, I don't believe He would have led me into that situation. However, I still have to be aware of my heart in moments of vulnerability because, in those times, I know I am more susceptible to fall. I then must readjust my boundary level accordingly to maintain wholeness and freedom. It's important to always remember that the boundary is not the goal, freedom is.

Love Never Fails

As we fall in love with the Christ who lives within us and draw our identity from Him instead of from our behaviors, we will discover a freedom to thrive in the midst of a dark world. We can give the people of the world a love encounter with Love Himself. He is the friend of sinners. We will understand that we are powerful and can overcome the powers of the world around us, and it will not depend on our own strength anymore. We are as holy and free as we believe that Christ has made us to be. We don't have to be bound by the pull of the world any longer. We are powerful to love the world in the face of adversity. Through freedom and wise boundaries, we are able to rise above our circumstances and be greater than the subordinate issues that oppose us.

We should stop trying so hard to earn God's pleasure. Instead, we should *rest* in His good pleasure towards us as His beloved children. This is who we are and what we are to Him. What is this Christianity thing really all about? Love. Simply, unconditional love. *"Love never fails"* (1 Corinthians 13:8). With love, all the other things work themselves out naturally.

18

The Power of Love

A religious man once asked Jesus, *"Teacher, which is the great commandment in the Law?"* And Jesus replied, *"'You shall love the Lord your God with all your heart, and with all your soul, and with all your mind.' This is the great and foremost commandment. The second is like it, 'You shall love your neighbor as yourself'"* (Matthew 22:36-39).

Then He summarized, *"On these two commandments hang all the Law and the Prophets"* (Matthew 22:40 NKJV). He was explaining that the entire Old Testament law is fulfilled by loving upward and loving outward. Any righteousness that a person aims to have in their actions must spring forth from love. The heart is the hub from where all our expressions flow. It is the source that produces behaviors and attitudes. This is why it is vital for us to understand the true nature of our heart—that it is now in union with Christ and no longer with the old, sinful nature. We are no longer the brood of vipers Jesus would have spoken about.

*"Either **make the tree good and its fruit good**, or make the tree bad and its fruit bad; for the tree is known by its fruit. You brood of vipers, how can you, being evil, speak what is good? **For the mouth speaks out of that which fills the heart. The good man brings out of his good treasure what is good**; and the evil man brings out of his evil treasure what is evil"* (Matthew 12:33-35). A heart that is filled with love is going to flow with love, causing good fruit to come out as a natural by-product.

The thing that we children of the Most High God have going for us is that He has already placed the good in our hearts. Jeremiah

31:33 prophesied of our current reality in Christ—"*But this is the covenant which I will make with the house of Israel after those days,' declares the Lord, 'I will put My law within them and on their heart I will write it; and I will be their God, and they shall be My people.'*" This is a New Covenant law that came after God canceled the authority of the Old Covenant law (see Colossians 2:14). Why would He choose to write His law on our hearts? Because it is a law of love instead of rules. There is no better place to inscribe the laws of love than on the human heart. He designed His laws to be perfectly fulfilled through the expression of true love.

> *Moreover, I will give you a new heart and put a new spirit within you; and I will remove the heart of stone from your flesh and give you a heart of flesh. I will put My Spirit within you and cause you to walk in My statutes, and you will be careful to observe My ordinances* (Ezekiel 36:26-27).

He didn't just place His laws on our hearts; He placed them on His heart and then exchanged hearts with us, disposing of our old one. "*Our old self was crucified with Him, in order that our body of sin* (i.e. heart of stone) *might be done away with…*" (Romans 6:6). He instilled His desires for godliness inside us. It is our true nature to want to do good. We are inclined for righteousness. He not only gave us His heart, He also gave us His Spirit to bring us into union with His desires. We have Christ within us living His life through us. "*It is no longer I who live, but Christ lives in me*" (Galatians 2:20). We just need to yield to this truth.

> *But I say, walk by the Spirit, and you will not carry out the desire of the flesh* (that old nasty sinful nature; heart of stone). *For the flesh sets its desire against the Spirit, and the Spirit against the flesh; for these are in opposition to one another, so that you may not do the things that you please. But if you are led by the Spirit, you are not under the Law* (Galatians 5:16-18).

Jesus also said, *"If you love Me, you will keep My commandments"* (John 14:15). Intimate connection with Jesus breeds holiness. When you are in love with someone, you are naturally inclined to do the things that please them, not the things that hurt them. Loving and blessing become second nature. My friend once told me of a pastor who said, "Love God and do as you please, because when you love God, you will do what pleases Him."

This means that we already have within us the complete ready-to-go package through our New Covenant union with Jesus Christ. It is like an M.R.E. (Meal Ready to Eat) in the army; you just add the water and dinner is on. We have the goods. All we have to do is add the love and holiness is on. It is amazing that God is not looking for me to do everything perfectly and to make no mistakes in trying. He is simply looking to see if my love is on. If I am loving Him, loving myself, and loving my neighbor well, all is good. It is my utmost desire to love God with my whole heart, soul, and mind. I truly want to exemplify Jesus to those around me by loving them as myself. These are, after all, the two greatest commandments in the Law.

More Love Needed

"If I could only love Jesus more….that is all that matters….I need to try to be more in love with Him…*Heart, I command you to increase in love now*! How can I prove my love to Him? Maybe I can worship Him more. Or maybe I can share His love with other people more. There is a world full of broken, empty souls who need me to love them. God needs to feel more love from me and to see it exhibited more through me. I need to give Him what He deserves, which is a lot more than what I have given to Him."

Beep! Beep! Beeeeeep!!! Beep! Beep! Beeeeeep!!!

What was that noise? Oh dang, it was my false-security alarm. It detects when I enter into works-mode in trying to make God happier with me. It indicates when I am searching for a sense of false security in my own abilities. Every time it goes off, I am reminded that I cannot perform for acceptance; I cannot earn His pleasure and love by trying hard enough. Even the commandment to love does not get it done. Yes, love is at the center of what God wants for us and has for us; but it is still law if we attempt to do it from the wrong source.

This may sound radical, but although loving God with all our heart, soul, and mind, and loving our neighbor as ourselves are the greatest commandments, they are still law if they are the starting point. There is actually something we need to do that is greater than these two commandments.

Greater than the Greatest Commandments

First John 4:19 says, "*We love Him because He first loved us*" (NKJV). If we want to love God well, there is something greater we need. We need to first *know* and *receive* His love for us. Most Christians experience the abounding expressions of God's love for a season after they accept Jesus into their lives. Unfortunately, many people eventually shift their love experience from recipient to donor, believing that they have to pay God back for what He has done for them. They spend the rest of their lives trying hard to live for God. Their efforts were initiated by a true love that honored God deeply. However, when people's love for God becomes generated by fading memories of an intimacy they once had, they tend to forget what love really looks like and how to do it properly. It is high time that we all get back to the basics.

Christianity 101: **God is love** (see 1 John 4:16). Love is the gateway that gets us into the Kingdom, and it is the rite of passage that promotes us further in the Kingdom. If we ever feel that we have advanced to greater levels than *Jesus Loves Me, This I Know*, then we have "taken a wrong turn in Albuquerque," as Bugs Bunny would say, and ended up in Antarctica among "the frozen chosen." Anybody who has gone beyond the fundamental element of what Christianity is all about has not built line upon line, precept upon precept. They have built a castle on a sand foundation, and a tsunami is quickly approaching the shore. It is a tidal wave of God's love. Will they know what hit them?

If this is you, then hear the message of Jesus Christ. "*But I have this against you, that you have left your first love. Therefore remember from where you have fallen, and repent and do the deeds you did at first"* (Revelation 2:4-5). Notice that the problem has nothing to do with works or behaviors; it has to do with love. The time is now, not later. Jesus is making it very clear to us that if our Christianity ever gets into something other than a love affair with Him, it is no longer any good. If love encounters are a mere nostalgic memory of the past, it is time to "get back to Albuquerque" and find out where you can make that heart connection again. Jesus is storing His love like liquid in a container whose brim is the continental shoreline, and He is waiting to dump it all over you.

Perhaps you find it difficult to identify with the references that we, as children of the King, are seated in the heavenly places in our holy union with Jesus. Maybe this difficulty is because of a lack of the revelation of this truth. But is it possible that it is because you may have lost some of that fiery love which was once in your heart for Him? Revelation 3:14-22 speaks of Christians who have lost their passion for Jesus and have resorted to self-sufficiency in their Christian lifestyles. If this is you, He is calling you to repentance in the form of opening your heart wide and receiving His intimacy. He says, *"Behold, I stand at the door and knock; if anyone hears My voice and opens the door, I will come in to him and will dine with him, and he with Me"* (Revelation 3:20).

We have the power to overcome a lukewarm heart by responding to His request for entry into the heart, as He brings intimate love and holy union with Him. You see, Jesus is not standing there with His arms crossed and a frown, waiting for you to love Him well enough. He is eagerly knocking on the door of your heart trying to bring the headwaters of love in. Our reception of His love is the love action He is seeking. That is what makes our hearts hot instead of lukewarm or cold.

Desiring Jesus and drawing on this intimate heart connection with Him is how we overcome. *"But in all these things we overwhelmingly conquer through Him who loved us"* (Romans 8:37). Overcoming a lukewarm heart by becoming completely dependent upon His love yields great rewards and manifests our inheritance and true identities.

It is what brings us into heavenly encounters where we are seated with Him. In Revelation 3:21, Jesus proceeded to say to the lukewarm Christians, *"He who overcomes, I will grant to him to sit down with Me on My throne, as I also overcame and sat down with My Father on His throne."* It is an Ephesians 2:6 reality—"(He has) *seated us with Him in the heavenly places in Christ Jesus."* It doesn't happen by our efforts, but by embracing His love.

God isn't very interested in what we offer Him if it is not an expression of love and adoration (see 1 Corinthians 13:1-3). If you want to love God more, then get a revelation of how deep His love is for you. We can only love God in direct proportion to how much we believe He loves us. We are vessels. If we aren't filled up, we have nothing to pour out. The fuller we are, the more we can pour. We love God by pouring love back onto Him, because His love becomes our love. You can only give away what you already have.

Love Thy Neighbor

If you want to do a better job at loving your neighbor as yourself, there are two things that must happen. The first is accomplished by capturing a greater revelation of Jesus' extravagant love for you. Again, you can only give away according to what you already have.

The second thing is accomplished by loving yourself. Jesus said that we are supposed to love our neighbor as ourselves. A lot of people don't love themselves very much. Religion deceives many people into believing it is prideful and self-centered to love themselves. Some people are insecure because of a lack of confidence, be it in self or in Christ; thus they don't love themselves well. Regardless of why people may not love themselves, it is a commandment from God.

God's expectation of the way we should love our neighbor is much higher than the way some people "love" themselves. But when God talks about love, He always refers to His infinite, abounding love that is so big and powerful that even He cannot withhold it. The love He wants the world around us to encounter is not meager; it is radical. It is the kind that makes the Creator of the Universe dethrone Himself to die a criminal's death in man's place and then adopt them as His royal heirs.

God wants us to exhibit His love in its fullest expression. But He says that we can only properly love our neighbor to the degree that we love ourselves. If you want to win the world to Jesus, start by winning your own heart to Him first.

Commercial airlines are required by law to teach safety regulations before each flight begins. I have flown so many times that it has become white noise. The main thing I still try to make sure I listen for is when I'm sitting in an exit row and they ask me if I agree to the terms for assisting in rescue in the event of a crash.

But one thing I have noticed in their routine speech is the warning that, if we should hit enough turbulence that the oxygen masks drop, we are to first take care of ourselves before helping others. The idea behind this is that you are no good for helping other people if you are choking and losing oxygen to your brain. The first oxygen mask should go on your face. If once you have made sure your survival needs are taken care of, then you will have the strength and focus to help many others more effectively. The moral? Help others by first helping yourself.

Let Jesus come and pour His love into your thirsty heart. Let Him keep pouring until it fills to the brim. Let Him keep filling until the only way for it to expand is by seeping through the walls of your being. Let it keep seeping until you reach complete saturation. Let it saturate until it oversaturates and has to spill out of your pores and overflow in every direction. If you want to love your neighbor as yourself, share your personal love encounter with them. Give them a big ol' taste of the goodness of God from which you have been drinking. Forget the tavern; this is the kind of drink that the world is dying for.

The level of experiential revelation of the love of God that you live in determines the level your neighbors will experience through you. It is no longer about scrounging up enough love to make a difference in somebody's life; it is about abiding in love and bringing others into your encounter. Let your ministry and calling simply happen from the spillover of basking in the euphoric atmosphere of God's rich, ecstatic love. When we are so filled with the love of Jesus, we find that we cannot help but to love those people around us. Compassion becomes our breath.

19

Recipe for Greater Love Encounters

You may be asking how you can bring yourself into a greater level of the experiential revelation of God's love? That is a great question. I will not attempt to give an exhaustive list of answers, as there are probably many more ways to approach it. I will, however, share three important ingredients to a love potion that I've discovered is guaranteed, when used with sincerity, to woo the presence of God right to you.

Ingredient #1: *Desperation*

I read a saying once that said, "A hungry man is an angry man." I would prefer to change it to say, "A hungry man is a desperate man." Some definitions of the word *desperate* refer to hopelessness, giving the sense that what is needed is not available. That is not the kind of desperation that moves God, because *"without faith it is impossible to please Him"* (Hebrews 11:6). I am referring to a kind of desperation like this: *"1.) having an urgent need, desire; 2.) extreme or excessive; 3.) making a final, ultimate effort; giving all"* (excerpt from www.dictionary.reference.com). There is an appropriate kind of desperation that urgently needs something so badly that one will do whatever it takes to have it, believing that it will happen. It is like extreme hunger or thirst, knowing one will die without the need being met.

God will always spot a heart that is hungry for Him. He discovered young, obscure David among an entire nation because he was "a man after His own heart" (1 Samuel 13:14). David was desperate for God's heart, and it drew God's attention. Blind Bartimaeus stopped Jesus in His tracks as He was en route to fulfill some eternally scheduled appointments in Jerusalem, because he needed a touch from God (see Mark 10:46-52). The Canaanite woman earnestly persuaded Jesus to extend His blessing beyond the racial boundaries of His mission (see Matthew 15:22-28). The woman with the issue of blood made Jesus too late to save Jairus's daughter because of her desperate, illegal attempt to touch His garment (see Luke 8:41-49). The desperation of these humble people altered Jesus' plans so He could fill their need.

Perhaps this is a good time to do a quick litmus test. Let's see how our desperation levels rank. Are they pH (profuse Hunger) balanced? The higher the "hunger-for-Christ's-love" rating spikes above the next highest ranking hunger, the more susceptible you are to the influences of His love. *"Blessed are those who hunger and thirst for righteousness, for they shall be satisfied"* (Matthew 5:6). God loves to satisfy a hungry and thirsty soul when it yearns for the goods that He provides.

He is moved by passion and honor. The more we want something from Him, the more He sees that we are fit to carry it. God wants to lavish us with His abounding love, but He manifests it to us according to how much we want it and how faithfully we will handle it. He is tender-hearted. He generally chooses to reveal His precious, intimate secrets in proportion to the measure that He can trust that we will honor and treasure them. The value we place on the things of God is what determines how much He feels is safe to share with us. It is not God's plan to restrain us from experiencing the full measure of His goodness. But it is our responsibility to accept the invitations by moving His heart with our desperation.

Ingredient #2: *Faith*

Now faith is the substance of things hoped for, the evidence of things not seen (Hebrews 11:1 NKJV).

Do you want to have a greater love encounter with God than what you are experiencing right now? Believe that there is a substance of what you are hoping for that is already present. Maybe what you await is invisible and intangible at this stage. But believe that it is there.

Faith understands that my answers already exist with God in the spirit realm. They only need to be transferred through the veil and manifested into the physical realm. Faith is the maternal force that gives birth to a conceived dream and brings it into the experiential realm. It knows that good is coming before it is able to be seen. When the void between our need and the provision is filled with faith, it becomes a tractor beam that pulls the targeted heavenly substance into the earthly sphere that we live in.

The amazing thing about faith is that, although it sounds like it is a lot of work to pull things from the other side of the veil to this side, it actually happens by rest. Yes, there are times for intercessory prayer and contending by pulling on the heavens, but even that shouldn't be done by striving.

Faith is not our ability to convince God that He should do something good, as if it was our idea first. Rather, faith is our ability to rest in His strong, gentle hands, trusting that He is good and faithful. It receives what He has already done and is already doing. If this ever comes with difficulty, remembering ways that He has been faithful in the past can always encourage our faith to trust and to rest in peace.

We all know that it is *"by grace you have been saved through faith; and that not of yourselves, it is the gift of God; not as a result of works, so that no one may boast"* (Ephesians 2:8-9). We have already talked thoroughly about the amazing grace of God and what it does for us. It is the unmerited, abounding favor of God; and it is the unlimited empowerment by God. It is by grace that we have been saved. Many miss the full understanding of this verse in thinking that it refers merely to how we became born again and saved out of sin. It includes that but a whole lot more.

The Greek word for "saved" is *sozo*. This word means more than just eternal security in Heaven. It refers to the all-encompassing, all-inclusive salvation of God. It is being rescued and restored in spirit, soul, and body, and in any other need one may have. (You can find different examples of how *sozo* is interpreted in the following verses: Matthew 1:21 – "to save from sins;" Matthew 9:21 – "to get well;" Matthew 14:30 – "to rescue from trouble;" Luke 8:36 – "to deliver from evil spirits.") *Sozo* refers to the unlimited provision of God where the need is lacking. Let me rephrase Ephesians 2:8: *"For by unmerited favor and divine empowerment* (grace) *you have been thoroughly rescued, restored, healed, and provided for* (saved) *through faith."*

God's grace flows outward bountifully and continually. It is immeasurable in volume, eternal in endurance, limitless in love. His grace never gets stronger or weaker because it is impossible to fluctuate an infinite virtue. Everywhere grace goes, light shines and joy abounds. Everything it lands on springs forth in life and melts internally with love.

GN=S. Salvation (*sozo*) is the chemical reaction that happens when Grace and Need fuse together. What is your need of the moment? Grace is your source of provision. Salvation is the manifestation of the need being met in full. Spiritual salvation is God meeting our need of being set free from bondage to the old sinful nature and restored into the nature of Christ. Physical salvation is God meeting our need for healing in the physical body and making it whole. Salvation of the soul is God meeting our need for restoration in the mind, will, and emotions. There are unlimited ways God meets our needs through salvation by grace.

When we don't see the manifestation of our need met in full, then that is where faith comes in. Faith is the substance that fills the gap until the answer arrives. Faith is what draws the answer in. It is what recognizes that God extravagantly provides for all of our needs. *"In Him we have redemption through His blood, the forgiveness of our trespasses, **according to the riches of His grace which He lavished on us"*** (Ephesians 1:7-8). Faith accepts what already is. It is not in striving; it is in resting in what already is. It is opening wide and drinking it in.

The Forecast for Today Is Clear Skies

Let me give a word picture for how I perceive the way faith works. I really enjoy a nice, bright day outside, especially when it doesn't exceed 100 degrees Fahrenheit. The sun is always shining brightly, impartial to where its rays end up. Its light is shining constantly, infinitely, eternally. In every direction it is shining. Its rays are a vital and primary element necessary to bring life and health to all living organisms. It brings joy and it makes people's day. It heats the atmosphere to a temperature that makes it possible for life to survive, thrive, and reproduce more life. Its rays go anywhere they are allowed to go. They bring the same resources with them to each cubic inch they travel, and they leave a continuous trail of light as far as they have permission to travel.

The only thing that can stop the sun's rays from bringing their gifts of life and joy is something that stands in the way. Light will not force its way through the barrier; but it will continue pushing forward against it with consistent energy. It is trying to bless what is behind the barrier, but it will not violate the position of what it is up against. It doesn't knock it down, nor does it try to find a detour. It stubbornly travels only straight; and it respects whatever stands in its path.

However, the moment that the barrier is removed, light shines on past its former halted location as though nothing were ever in its way. Light travels 186,000 miles per second. It doesn't like to wait to get to its destination, and it takes instant advantage when it gains the rite of passage. It pushes against that barrier waiting for it to open the same way as when I am stuck at a railroad crossing waiting for that arm to lift up. Once the sunlight's passage is open, everything that was in the dark and shriveled up from light deprivation begins to be restored. Life can spring forth and gain the strength to be vibrant and happy again.

You and I are like a house in the sun. Grace is radiating out from God's heart continually, omni-directionally, and impartially, being sent to wherever it may land. It is pressing up against the walls of the house, trying to get in. However, if the windows are covered by blinds and curtains, the light will not penetrate and cannot bring the goods of the abundant life and joy with salvation. It is available and ready to come in and fill the entire house the very moment the shades are opened. One hundred eighty-six thousand miles per second is slow compared to how instant Jesus wants to shed the light of His grace within our open hearts.

What is faith? Faith is simply opening the blinds to give the Light of the World the rite of passage. It is allowing the grace that is already pressing up against you to flow in and do what it is already doing. True faith does not exhaust itself by trying really hard to believe for something that is beyond you. It simply believes that He is already doing it. Faith is being able to rest as you give Him permission to come in and do what He already wants to do.

Where exhaustion may come in is when we have to work hard at renewing our minds away from believing that God hasn't already provided the answers. So relax. Simply receive the fact that God is bestowing upon you *unmerited favor* and *divine empowerment* (grace). And because of this, *you have been thoroughly rescued, restored, healed, and provided for through faith* (salvation).

Faith is simply believing and receiving what is already present in spiritual form. It is resting in that reality until we see it manifested in tangible form. Depending on what we are believing for, it is not always instant, but we must not let go. If we find ourselves waning in our rest-filled faith, we should go to the Word and declare scriptures that bring truth to the circumstance because *"faith comes from hearing, and hearing by the word of Christ"* (Romans 10:17).

Therefore, as we all desire a greater revelation and encounter with the love of God, let us embrace the reality that it is present. Let us rest assured that the experience is staring us in the face. We need to open our hearts wide and let Him pour in His lavish grace.

God is love. His grace is the virtue of love being extended outward. A love encounter is God's salvation to a famished soul. Faith allows His love to pour in, bringing a radical love encounter where it is needed most.

Ingredient #3: *Comprehending*

Back to the love tonic recipe. The apostle Paul prayed, "*That He* (Father God) *would grant you, according to the riches of His glory, to be strengthened with power through His Spirit in the inner man, so that Christ may dwell in your hearts through faith; and that you, being rooted and grounded in love, **may be able to comprehend with all the saints what is the breadth and length and height and depth, and to know the love of Christ which surpasses knowledge**, that you may be filled up to all the fullness of God*" (Ephesians 3:16-19).

I believe that this richness of Christ's dwelling in our hearts is determined by our faith. If we want a stronger manifestation of His abiding presence within us, we need to believe for it. This passage says that we get strengthened with the power of the Holy Spirit in our inner man in accordance with the riches of His glory. God's glory is mighty, powerful, infinite, and eternal. Nobody has done anything more than scratch the surface of the magnitude of His glory, including John the Revelator and Ezekiel the Prophet. Every aspect of who God is and every part of what He does is encompassed in His glory. Imagine the immense value of it. Consider the unfathomable amount of treasures and mysteries His glory contains. Oh, the wonder! And to think that we are strengthened in spirit according to the riches of His glory. He invests a great deal into making sure our spirits are strong in the love of Christ.

If Christ dwells in our hearts, we are certainly rooted and grounded in love. Love is the foundation that our lives are built upon. As we are in love with Christ and full of the empowerment of the Holy Spirit in accordance with the riches of His glory, we are well equipped to comprehend what comes next. In the verses we just read, Paul prayed that we "*may be able to **comprehend** with all the saints what is the breadth and length and height and depth, and to know the love of Christ which **surpasses knowledge**.*" (See Ephesians 3:16-19.)

I was always boggled by this prayer, as it contains a pretty heavy paradox. Paul is praying for our ability to comprehend something that is infinite and surpasses knowledge. The love of Jesus is so huge and overwhelming that, again, nobody has ever done more than scratch its surface. Our finite minds cannot possibly comprehend something of unfathomable proportions. We can only grasp things that can be measured.

He talks about the breadth, length, height, and depth of the love of Christ. Extend your arms straight out from your sides and point. His love stretches to infinity and beyond in those directions. Reach one arm forward and point and one arm back (if possible) and point. His love stretches to infinity and beyond in those directions, too. Extend one arm above your head and point and one arm toward the floor and point. His love stretches…you guessed it…to infinity and beyond in those directions as well. Our minds cannot conceive the magnitude of those dimensions being filled with something. Even the perimeter of the universe is difficult to understand because there are no boundaries. That is the size of the love of Christ. And look at who is right in the very center of all of those infinite arrows pointing to the dimensions of His love. It's you, right in the center of His heart.

We can grasp the size of His love to some weak, imaginative level. But that still does not accurately comprehend the weight of this love filling our hearts in full. The love of Christ truly does surpass knowledge. We only know it in part. So when Paul prayed that we may be able to comprehend something that surpasses knowledge, I remained frustrated at the contradiction. That is, until the Holy Spirit revealed the deeper meaning of what Paul was really saying.

The Spirit led me to look up this word, "comprehend," in the Greek language. When I studied it, I gawked, as I realized the meaning took me somewhere much deeper than the typical English definition for "comprehend," which is "to understand." This word in the Greek is *katalambano*. *Katalambano* can mean to comprehend or understand, but it has a much fuller, richer meaning. It is defined as, *"to take eagerly, seize, possess, apprehend, attain, come upon, comprehend, find, obtain, perceive, overtake."*

An example of another verse that uses *katalambano* in this way is 1 Thessalonians 5:4. *"But you, brethren, are not in darkness, that the day would overtake* (katalambano) *you like a thief."* *Katalambano* is not merely a word about mental capacity. It is a word about dominion and overtaking. It is a word that calls us to *apprehend*, which means *"to take into custody; to arrest."* It is a word that contains power to take control of a situation.

The Lord was revealing to me that a better way to read this verse is: "(That you) *may be able to* **apprehend / to seize / to take into custody** *with all the saints what is the breadth and length and height and depth, and to know the love of Christ which surpasses knowledge"* (Ephesians 3:18-19). What does this mean? It means that He has empowered us by the Holy Spirit with an insurmountable ability to actually reach out and seize His love and bring it into custody within our hearts. In a sense, He has given us the authority to take dominion of His manifest love. It is ours for the taking, but we have to take it. It is ever available, but it must be subdued. I am not saying we are more powerful than the love of Jesus, but I *am* saying that it is patiently waiting to be captured, and we should do so aggressively.

You are a love encounter waiting to happen. His love is like a spring-loaded trap just itching to be set off. He is so tickled to lavish you with it that He almost cannot stand to wait any longer. He anticipates courageous pursuit by you, one with confident expectation of positive results. So get your desperation on and rise up in faith with your God-given authority to *katalambano* His manifest love. You will not be disappointed. You want it, and He is waiting. We may never fully understand the limits of His love. But we will be able to know by experience greater and greater measures of His infinite love as we *katalambano* one level at a time.

The Love Potion

Have you ever eaten a piece of cake that was baked without eggs? Or cookies where the baker forgot to add butter? One time, Jessica and I got to eat dinner at our dear friend's house (who will remain anonymous). She made some delicious, unique Mexican food. And for dessert, we were excited to have some of her special gluten-free chocolate chip cookies. They looked perfect. Golden brown, moist, and speckled with softly melted morsels of delectable bliss. I picked one of those luscious treats up and salivated as it approached my mouth. As soon as I bit into that disc-shaped confection, it vaporized into a dust cloud that filled the air. We all nearly sneezed. It was the sweetest puff of air I had ever tasted; but it didn't quite meet my expectations for a cookie. She forgot an important ingredient: butter. I then grabbed a second helping of tacos to supplement the stomach real estate I had reserved for dessert.

Desperation is a very important quality in our pursuit to a greater love encounter with Jesus. However, if we don't use all the necessary ingredients, we will end up dry and dusty. Many people attempt to pursue Him with desperation as a stand-alone ingredient. Be warned that the only thing desperation will create, if it remains the sole contribution, is loads of frustration. The only kind of desperation that will move God is the kind that is coupled with believing faith. Without faith, desperation is nothing more than a poverty mentality because it yearns for something that it believes is out of reach and undeliverable. It's like a donkey chasing that dang carrot.

Unbelieving desperation is hopeless. It makes people dig for something unattainable until they eventually exhaust, fall into their pit, and bury themselves in self-pity. Desperation is cruel if it is an isolated ingredient because God generally does not respond to self-pity. He responds to faith. I've experienced this too many times in my life and wouldn't wish it on anyone. Sadly, I've met all too many people who are desperate for a touch from God but think it will never come unless a prophet is sent to them from afar.

Desperation coupled with faith, on the other hand, is very attractive to God. He loves when someone needs Him with every fiber of his being and also has enough faith to believe that God just might be good enough to give him the desires of his heart. How must God feel when people do not believe that He is really that good? Perhaps misunderstood. Maybe frustrated. I am not completely sure, but I do know that it does not attract Him to us.

On the contrary, faith greatly pleases God. Desperation motivated by faith moves God to respond with gifts. *"But without faith it is im-*

*possible to please Him, for he who comes to God must **believe** that He is, and that **He is a rewarder of those who diligently seek Him**"* (Hebrews 11:6 NKJV). When we diligently seek His love with a faith that believes that we are going to encounter it, our reward will be exuberant. His love is already staring us in the face. We need to open ourselves and let Him reward our seeking hearts.

Diligently seeking the deeper levels of His loving heart does not need to be a long, drawn out pursuit with no rewards along the way. God is not into causing people to have weariness of soul. He is not cruel. *"Hope deferred makes the heart sick, but desire fulfilled is a tree of life"* (Proverbs 13:12). God does not withhold His manifest love from people who believe and seek it. He truly loves to fulfill the desires of our hearts and bring life to them.

He wants us to understand that He has actually given us the power and authority to lasso His heart and pull it in. If we will rise up in faith to *katalambano* His heart, He will be sure to reward us with a fresh wave of love. If you feel like you are getting nothing, then start by pulling an "I love you!" from Him until you actually believe it, because He is already saying it. If nothing else, *katalambano* a "You are my beloved son / daughter, in whom I am well pleased!" out of Him until it sinks into your heart. Prepare to be touched with love!

20

Lover of My Soul

Not many years ago, I was praying and soaking in the presence of God and had an incredible encounter with Jesus. I was lying on my back on the floor listening to "soaking" music and asking to see God's face. I felt the warm, liquid, electrifying anointing of the Holy Spirit pour down upon my entire being. I saw a vision of a door in the sky that opened up before me. Different things started coming out of the door. God was speaking through them to show me that He had been with me since the beginning of my life.

I saw the light of Glory before me. There were things in the light that appeared to be angels and large golden birds. Then I saw a golden throne. As the glory intensified, I realized I was looking at God's huge, majestic throne.

Jesus appeared before me, shining in white glory with golden hues. He was beautiful to behold as I stared in wonder. He came and grabbed both of my shoulders and held me as He stared into my face. Then He hugged me with a warm embrace. Leaning into my ear, Jesus whispered, "I love you! I'm so proud of you. I love you just like you are." That felt so good to my heart.

I have been discovering for a few years now that Jesus is a lot more in love with us than we realize. When I get between a rock and a hard place in life, I can always resort to this reality and find my peace and courage once again. When I try to conjure up courage and strength on my own, I tend to fall short, or I find myself buried in an anxious mess, aimlessly trying to prove myself. But when I know I am loved by someone who means the world to me, I can conquer the world with nothing

UNCONDITIONAL: LIBERATED BY LOVE

to prove. (I especially feel that way with my wife and with Jesus.) God is no respecter of persons and shows no partiality in His expressions of love (see Romans 2:11). You see, Jesus is proud of me and loves me just like I am. He feels the same way towards you, too!

The Disciple Whom Jesus Loved

The following revelation is one I received by the inspiration of Chris Gore, Pastor of Bethel Church Healing Rooms. Have you ever noticed that Jesus had a follower who was often referred to as "the disciple whom Jesus loved"? It is fascinating that out of all the 12 disciples, only one took this title. And it wasn't the obvious man, to whom Jesus said, "*I also say to you that you are Peter, and upon this rock I will build My church; and the gates of Hades will not overpower it*" (Matthew 16:18), who went on to become the leading apostle to the Jews. No, it was the man who edged his way nearest to Jesus' heart as he made it his custom to lean upon His breast at supper (see John 21:20). His name was John.

Jesus is moved by anyone who is eager to edge their way nearest to His heart. He loves people regardless; however, He reserves a special kind of intimacy for those who cherish it most—the kind that lets you in on the secrets of His heart. It was the disciple whom Jesus loved, the one who risked it all to get in closer than anyone else, who ended up having the greatest revelation of the resurrected, glorified Christ ever recorded in human history. The journals of this experience became the closing statement of God's New Covenant. It is called the Book of Revelation.

Radical love encounters inspire boldness, courage, and strength to endure the hardest circumstances that we may ever face. When Jesus was betrayed into the hands of His executors, all of His disciples stumbled. Only John returned to Jesus and did not abandon Him when everyone else did. John's intimate relationship with the Lord gave him the strength to stand before Jesus' ugly, bloody, shredded body hanging on the cross, while knowing that he, John, could be captured and tortured too.

186

John *had* been captured, but in a completely different way. Jesus trusted His beloved so much that He entrusted His mother into John's care. This was a relationship that nothing could tear apart. It was a depth that all His disciples needed, but only the one discovered.

The thing that is fascinating about John and his title as "the disciple whom Jesus loved" is the fact that it is only mentioned in one book of the Bible. Can you guess which one? Matthew didn't mention it, and neither did Mark or Luke. It was mentioned in the Gospel according to John, authored by none other than John himself. He gave himself the title. It reminds me of the verse claiming Moses as the most humble man on the face of the Earth, written in Numbers 12:3—a book Moses wrote.

Is this arrogance? Not in the least. It is confidence. John knew who he was to Jesus because he huddled close to His heart. He knew what Jesus thought of Him. He was well acquainted with the love of Jesus that goes much deeper than mere words. It was a covenant relationship of deep trust. It was a bond that gave him access to ask the hard questions that the other disciples wouldn't dare ask (see John 13:24-25). Jesus loved John deeply, and John knew this love.

With the knowledge of His love comes special privileges that you just cannot receive without it. Through his encounters with the love of Jesus, John gained such an intimate revelation that he wrote four of the most profound books on the subject, each bearing his own name. A few of the quotes from his books say such things as:

For God so loved the world, that He gave His only begotten Son, that whoever believes in Him shall not perish, but have eternal life (John 3:16).

The one who does not love does not know God, for God is love (1 John 4:8).

See how great a love the Father has bestowed on us, that we would be called children of God; and such we are… (1 John 3:1).

John knew the love of God and it transformed his life. It made him a different breed. The intimacy he had with Jesus gave him a profound worldview, a bird's eye perspective from Heaven to Earth. He understood the teachings of Jesus well. He wrote about abiding in the Vine, drawing life from Jesus, and bearing the fruit of love through this intimate union (see John 15). John discovered the union that is available in the heavenly places.

You and I are also offered the privilege of entering into deeper levels of intimacy with Jesus Christ. Actually, we should go ahead and accept this invitation from the entire Holy Trinity. How about we respond to it until we can acknowledge that we, too, are the "disciples whom Jesus loves"?

Kisses From Heaven

I remember one period of time when the Lord was bringing me into a special season of radical intimacy with Himself. I was learning some new concepts about the Holy Spirit that I didn't quite understand at the time. One of my closest friends, David Jonas, taught me some principles that took my relationship with God to a whole new level. The Holy Spirit is the part of the Trinity who is actually physically present on this Earth in full form right now. Of course, the whole Godhead is omnipresent, all places at all times. But there is something special about the way that the Spirit is here.

The Holy Spirit is a lover. He is tender-hearted and can be easily grieved. But on the flipside, He can also be easily wooed when He knows that the heart of whom is charming Him is sincere. I began practicing this by being more intentional with worshiping Him directly. He is just as worthy of worship as the rest of the Godhead. I found ways to speak adorations to Him and tell Him how beautiful and wonderful He is.

I would let love songs, poetry, and words of adoration flow out of my heart; things like: "Oh, how I love Your presence, Holy Spirit! It melts my heart and transforms me more into the image of Christ. Your nearness makes me more like Jesus. It's who You are that does

this to me. You are so holy! I love You and need You more than ever!"
I can feel His response to this even as I type this worship right now.
Praise You, Holy Spirit! You are worthy!

If you ever want to experience more of the manifest presence of
God, woo the Holy Spirit. It attracts Him so much. The wonderful
part is that He never comes without love, joy, peace, or any of the
other fruits of the Spirit. The fruits are actually the very essence of
His nature; they are His personality (see Galatians 5:22-23). He will
bring you into a love affair that you will never want to leave. But it
needs to be cultivated and stewarded if you desire to maintain it and
deepen it.

One morning as I was awoke, I began expressing adoration to the
Holy Spirit. I was practicing what I learned from Benny Hinn in *Good
Morning, Holy Spirit*. It was as if He was standing in the corner just
waiting patiently for me to wake up. Instantly, I felt His presence
begin swirling all around me like a mini-hurricane in my bedroom.
He was moved by my expressed love. I am not exaggerating, but I literally felt Him physically come right in front of my face and grab it.
Then I felt His face press up against mine. He pressed His lips up
against my lips and gave me a big kiss. Remaining on my mouth was
what felt like a residue of electrified anointing oil. I was blown away
by this response. He really does love me. He adores me!

There is controversy over whether the Song of Solomon was written as a prophetic parable of Jesus Christ's relationship as Husband to
the Bride (the Church) or as a love story for couples who celebrate
romance in the institution of earthly marriage. The answer is YES!
Why not both? If you read Ephesians 5:22-33 carefully, you will learn
that the parallel between Jesus' relationship to the Church and the
husband's relationship to the wife is identical in nature, and you can
learn principles about one by evaluating the other. With that said, I
have discovered some profoundly helpful hints to our love life with
Jesus in the Song of Solomon.

Remember what I said happened to me that morning when I woke
up? The Shulamite (Solomon's wife) prophesied of this: "***May he kiss
me with the kisses of his mouth!*** *For your love is better than wine*"

(Song of Solomon 1:2). He really does kiss us with the kisses of His mouth. His kisses may or may not come in literal form like this, but He is giving kisses out to His loved ones all the time. We need only to pay attention enough to recognize when they come and give Him an appropriate response.

"*Every good thing given and every perfect gift is from above, coming down from the Father of lights, with whom there is no variation or shifting shadow*" (James 1:17). What good things has He done for you lately? They are kisses from Heaven. He is more in love with you than you know!

I don't want to be weird in trying to get too detailed with what it means for Jesus to be the Husband and us the Bride; but it is a picture of His utmost intimacy and *hesed* (covenant-loyalty love). He chose us; we didn't choose Him. Why? Because He wants our hearts so badly. So—we have the liberty to receive the benefits of what He is already bringing us. Woo Him and pucker up!

(I understand that the idea of God kissing you or being intimate with you can create confusion and discomfort when thinking of Him as a mere human man. But let us elevate our perspective on this and make sure to realize that God is not a man, and is not even male or female. He is God; He is Divine; He is Love; and He is pure. Let us not rob ourselves of divine fulfillment because of inferior perspectives that create awkwardness.)

Sweeter Than Wine, Part 1

May he kiss me with the kisses of his mouth! **For your love is better than wine** (Song of Solomon 1:2).

His love is better than wine. Why would the Shulamite compare love with wine? I will tell you why. When we drink in the manifest love of Jesus, it can become intoxicating. Love is not meant to just be a concept. It is meant to be an experience, a way of life. It is potent and can overwhelm a thirsty soul.

Recently, I led a team of Bethel students on a mission trip to Japan.

We were ministering and sowing into the hunger for revival in the Japanese churches. On our first night of ministry, the Holy Spirit broke out in a very explosive way, filling people fresh with His presence and releasing joyous, holy laughter across the room. The glory was very precious among us that night. Some people couldn't even stand up. Sensing His holiness, I felt a conviction to choose carefully what and how I spoke so I wouldn't quench the Holy Spirit.

After the meeting was over, a Japanese friend came to tell me of a unique way God manifested Himself that night of which I was unaware. During a moment when I was praying in tongues, she overheard me say a word in the Japanese language. It's important to understand that I only know a couple of phrases in Japanese, and this was not one of them. I didn't even realize that my tongue sounded Asian.

She told me that I said *Sakedokoro*. I learned that this word has dual meaning. "The first meaning," she explained, "is *secret place*, or *hiding place*." Later that evening, I was reflecting on this cool experience with my host family. They taught me that in Psalm 32:7, where it says, "You are my hiding place," in the Japanese Bible, it says, "You are my *sakedokoro*." I was amazed that, through a prophetic tongue in their own language, God was beckoning us to pursue Him in the secret place.

That in itself was powerful enough. However, it went to a completely different level of awesome when the lady explained the other meaning of this word. "*Sakedokoro* also means *house of wine*," she said. It was interesting to learn that the town we were in, called Nishinomiya, is famously nicknamed *Sakedokoro* because it is a special place for rice wine, or sake. I immediately understood that God was being poetically prophetic in His use of the dual meanings. He was revealing the key to His heart. The invitation to intimacy with Jesus in the secret place is an invitation to encounter the manifest affections of His love.

Love is a benefit from which we can drink. Ephesians 5:18 tells us of another—"*Do not get drunk with wine, for that is dissipation, but be filled with the Spirit*." God does not want us to waste our time falling under the influence of alcohol because He has something much better for us than that. Getting filled with the Holy Spirit is so much more powerful than wine or Jack Daniels and is much more constructive and redemptive. Those other things can be counterfeits to the real thing that God is dishing out.

On the Day of Pentecost, the Holy Spirit fell upon the disciples, and they were baptized in His power. When the Holy Spirit falls on people, strange things can happen to them, making them seem "not so normal." When He fell on the disciples, they became what some have termed "drunk in the Spirit." The manifestation of their baptism in the Spirit apparently had some intoxicating side effects to it. The crowds of people surrounding them thought they were plastered and made fun of them, saying, *"They are full of sweet wine."* Peter stood up and replied, *"These men are not drunk, as you suppose"* (Acts 2:15) and then proceeded to explain to them that this was the effect of the outpouring of the Holy Spirit, which was prophesied by Joel. They weren't drunk as the people supposed; they were drinking a whole different kind of substance.

There are a lot of people who have been baptized in the Holy Spirit. But the question I would ask is if they have been continually filled with the Holy Spirit. A one-time experience makes for a great memory where one could build a shrine. What happened years ago was amazing! But if it didn't continue to stay fresh and to increase, it was not the full experience God intended. Intimacy deepens from continuously breathing the Holy Spirit like oxygen.

I love to be filled fresh with the Holy Spirit. It is always exhilarating and often intoxicating. I know of no better way to describe it than being inebriated under the influence of the ecstatic bliss of His holy presence.

The Holy Spirit is the One who is responsible for causing love encounters to happen to us. Romans 5:5 says, *"And hope does not disappoint, because the love of God has been poured out within our hearts through the Holy Spirit who was given to us."* It is crucial that we cultivate a deeper level of intimacy with the Holy Spirit if we want more divine love encounters.

Hopefully, now it is making more sense for how wine is such an effective element of comparison. We have the opportunity to get "intoxicated" by two virtues: God's love and the fresh infilling of the Holy Spirit. It really is impossible to have one without the other.

The Shulamite's friends said, "*We will be glad and rejoice in you. We will remember your love more than wine*" (Song of Solomon 1:4 NKJV).

Here again is a reference to the love of God being compared with wine. This song of romance has no problem describing the euphoria of love in such exotic language. Even Nora Jones gets this concept in her song, *Don't Know Why*. She serenades, "My heart is drenched in wine. You'll be on my mind forever." This is how I feel about Jesus.

The Shulamite went further to say, "*He has brought me to his banquet hall, and his banner over me is love*" (Song of Solomon 2:4).

The Hebrew word for "banquet" is *Yayin* and means "wine; intoxication." The Hebrew word for "hall" is *Bayith* and means "house." What this literally means is, "*He has brought me into His **house of wine**, and His banner over me is love*." Jesus proudly waves His banner over us as He pours out His love like wine, overwhelming us in His lavish goodness. He loves to bring us into His cellar loaded with fine vintage. It is one way that He proudly proclaims His love over us. And this language is directly from the Bible.

Am I saying that you have to be in a boozed up slosh-fest if you want to encounter the extravagant love of God? Of course not. I'm not saying we should act foolish or look ridiculous and call it God. The main idea I want to convey is that His love is something wonderful that we can receive with a similar level of effort to taking a drink of liquid. It is not difficult to draw it in when we really believe it is present. And furthermore, I hope to convey that this spiritual liquid we get to ingest is loaded with the benefits of goodness which release the virtues of love, peace, joy, strength, courage, soundness of mind, healing, and many other wonderful life-enriching qualities.

Whether you find yourself interested in the concept of intoxication or not, I just hope that you will get the idea that His love is a power that has the ability to fill you. It will become absorbed into your blood and influence your behaviors and mindsets. It brings a great deal of joy and peace with it. It cuts off the edge of stress and fear. Actually, it casts them out completely. *"There is no fear in love; but perfect love casts out fear..."* (1 John 4:18). Love inspires courage that is beyond natural. The love of God is beautiful and powerful. It can change someone's demeanor in a very positive way. It is more exhilarating than anything I have ever experienced. I prefer this over alcohol or drugs any day. It certainly has better side effects!

Warning: Side Effects Are Likely

Consider the kinds of feelings you have experienced in the presence of God. There are countless manifestations people may feel when they encounter God. Butterflies in the stomach, goose bumps, the feeling of oil pouring over the head and body, electricity, numbness, heat, fire, cold chills, wind blowing, tingling, light-headedness, feelings of drunkenness without alcohol, loss of strength, shaking, belly laughing, crying, deep groaning, the feeling of an invisible, weighty presence sitting upon you. These are just a few common physical manifestations I have experienced or have heard that other people commonly experience. It is obviously not an exhaustive list.

If you read some of those manifestations that you haven't experienced, they may or may not sound pleasant or desirable based on the short description. But let me just say that they are experienced with peace, joy, exhilaration, and utmost love. When God touches His beloved, it is always a blessing that becomes addictive.

It may happen to the entire body or just in small parts. It may happen on the outside of the body or on the inside. It may happen in dynamic ways, or it may be so subtle that you barely recognize it is there. (I am not suggesting that every time you are feeling these feelings that they are coming from God, either. You may just be working too close to a power line. I am also not suggesting that they have to come at all during a love encounter.) Have you ever felt any of these sensations in any measure when a worship song, a scripture, a testimony, or a thought about God touched your heart in a special way? If so, that was an encounter of the Holy Spirit pouring the love of God, which is better than wine, upon you. It is best to just believe it and let it happen.

Perhaps you have never felt a physical touch of God. That is okay and does not disqualify you from being amazing in the eyes of God. It is not beneficial to judge others or ourselves based on our tangible experiences with God. He is unique in how He handles each of His loved ones. Just as important, and probably more, are the internal manifestations that come from His presence.

I often feel a deep peace filling me up, which causes all stress and fear to dissipate in His presence. He is, after all, the Prince of Peace. Joy comes and fills hearts that couldn't laugh well before. Courage rises up to face intimidating giants. Trust in God's goodness and faithfulness gets reestablished. Clarity of mind is restored. Wisdom and vision are gained. Refreshing of strength and restoration of soul are given. There is so much more to gain in His presence.

So many wonderful things happen in the presence of God. It is impossible for a lover of Jesus to come into His manifest presence and not be radically transformed in some needed way. Whatever your recognizable experience was, that was a kiss from Heaven. It is very important to pay attention to how He is trying to administer His heart to you. Whatever He did, it was the love of God being poured out on you through the Holy Spirit. He was blessing you with a love encounter. When you experienced that goodness, it was His banner of love over you, inviting you into the deeper recesses of His wine cellar. When we experience His goodness in any measure, He has given us the opportunity to *katalambano* more and more. His storehouse is unlimited, and He is yearning for us to pursue the more.

Some Christians don't want to allow the manifestations that come with God's presence into their lives or their churches. That is unfortunate for them because they are missing out on something wonderful that is just as available to them as anyone else. Some people don't like the way it looks because it appears foolish. But when you are smitten with love, you are willing to look foolish in your expressions. It can make you act like Buddy the Elf when he interrupted his dad's important business meeting to announce, "I'm in love! I'm in love! And I don't care who knows it!" The more we abandon our image, our security of social status, or fears of the unknown to allow ourselves the right to be smitten by God's love, the more we will be smitten.

David certainly was not concerned about his appearance when he celebrated the restoration of the shekinah glory to Israel while bringing back the Ark of the Covenant from exile. His wife, Michal, scorned him for dancing like a fool in his underwear before the entire nation. David was so in love with God that he cared only about God's praise and not his own. He responded, "*...I will play [music] before the LORD. And I will be even more undignified than this, and will be humble in my own sight...*" (2 Samuel 6:21-22 NKJV).

Some people are afraid of the manifestations of His presence because they don't want to lose control. However, when we are in the presence of the Almighty, who is really in control? Not you and not me. This fear of losing control is a sign of mistrust in God. It reveals that we think He may not have it in His heart or His ability to bring us into the blessings that we need and desire. But He does nothing except bless and improve us when we release our grip on life and float on His love, letting Him do to us as He pleases. That is utmost faith. Believe it or not, it is possible to be *in order* and be *wrecked* simultaneously by the love of Jesus. Usually God's idea of "order" is different than ours.

God has more for us than what we are currently experiencing. Imagine the limitless amount of opportunities that we have to experience the fullness of God. Whatever your best encounter in life ever was, multiply it by 1000 and that is still weak compared to what He wants to do with you. The fullness of God is so far beyond our control. How much do you want?

Let us make the decision to "let go and let God" when it comes to love encounters and receiving the outpouring of the Holy Spirit on our lives. Let us stop concerning ourselves with whether or not going all in will make us look like fools. Why shouldn't we be fools for Jesus anyway? Let's trust that "*God has chosen the foolish things of the world to shame the wise, and God has chosen the weak things of the world to shame the things which are strong"* (1 Corinthians 1:27). Let us trust that God will bring only good things into our lives when we allow Him to come in and take complete control. Let us get over ourselves and take the plunge into Jesus' wine cellar. He wants us to discover being "the disciple whom Jesus loves." Let us come under the influence of His love in the presence of the Holy Spirit. God is my Sakedokoro! Cheers!

The One Petal Daisy

ife with God is incredibly amazing once we have discovered
the euphoria of His manifest love for us. The more we meditate on this revelation, the more we are cultivating His
manifest presence in our lives. The more we learn of how great His
love is for us, the more we are able to pour love of the same proportions back to Him, ourselves, and our neighbors. There is nothing
greater in this life than to know the depths and rewards of His love.

We love the benefits of His love being expressed to us. But
shouldn't we also wonder about the flip side of the coin? What is God
experiencing in this love affair? Is it just we who are living in this ec-
stasy? Does God only dish out the goods and not receive? I wonder
what the Lover of Our Souls gets to experience on His side of the union. I'm glad you asked. I want to attempt to give you the slightest
glimpse of that glorious reality (in which I still have much more to
discover).

Leap of Faith or Sleep of Faith?

Back in the mid '90s, I was 20 years old and attending World Harvest
Bible College in Columbus, Ohio. One Friday night, I got to hang out
with David Jonas (my friend mentioned in the previous chapter who
mentored me in the ways of the Holy Spirit) and a couple of his friends.
We went over to one of their houses for dinner and a movie. I don't
know how I did it, but I was able to secure the couch for my own personal relaxation and movie viewing pleasures. It was a miracle because

I knew it was David's choice seat. God's favor must have been on me that night. Of all the movies they could have chosen for us to watch, they selected *Leap of Faith* with Steve Martin. A perfect training movie for revivalists-in-the-making... *not.*

By the time we got the movie started, it was already starting to get late. The movie probably wasn't more than half over by the time each and every one of us had conked out and were sawing logs. It may have been the movie that did it, or maybe the late hour, but I don't think so. We were all well adapted to staying up late in those days and to watching stupid movies. But sometimes God opens up a valve of holy anesthesia gas to put people to sleep when He is up to something delicate. He did it with Adam in Genesis 2 and with Abraham in Genesis 15. I think He did it with all of us that night too, because He was about to do something very delicate with me that changed my life forever.

My body was out cold on that cozy couch as I was lying on my back. That seems to be the position He often likes me in when I have mystical encounters. And that was what was about to happen. Although my body was asleep, my spirit woke right up at the commotion which stirred. The ceiling directly above me had just opened up into a portal from Heaven to Earth similar to what Jacob saw in Genesis 28. Through that portal descended the shekinah glory cloud of God and it rested upon me.

The Holy Spirit was in the cloud, hovering and brooding. He fluttered up and down my entire being. My body was paralyzed and I couldn't move. I felt electrical vibrations pulsating through my entire body with a charge that probably radiated at least four feet out of my flesh as He was flowing in waves. From head to toe, toe to head, up and down, down and up. It was powerful! Magnificent! I cannot describe it in words that will give it justice. It was as if I could see Him, but I can't describe what He looked like. I felt like I was in the middle of a lightning cloud. The vibrations of His fluttering felt and sounded just like what I saw years later when I looked upon a white dove flapping its wings inside of a birdcage. It made sense to me how He appeared as a dove coming upon Jesus in the Jordan River.

As the Holy Spirit was zapping me in that cloud, someone else descended through Heaven's gate and landed to my left. He was none other than Jesus Christ in person. A few angels came accompanying Him. The Lover of My Soul was standing on the floor beside me! I could feel His tangible presence. Although I was paralyzed and couldn't turn my head to gaze upon Him, I could see a small portion of Him out of the corner of my eye. My flesh was asleep, but my spirit could see the lower portion of His left side as He faced me. Around Him was the light of His glory radiating from His robe.

I could sense the presence of the angels nearby; but Jesus had my undivided attention. He physically grabbed my left hand and began pouring His love into my being, as if it were a warm, flowing, liquid substance. I felt it and was getting filled up with the love. It was the most beautiful experience I had ever known. And then I heard His audible voice speak to me. It was profound.

"My Jesse... My Jesse... My Jesse," He said with a deep, soft voice. If He was never able to melt my heart before, it was butter on a furnace that night. His words were full of adoration and intimate love for me.

You see, He was responding to my heart's cry. I had been heartsick for Jesus. It was often in those days when I would lock myself alone in a room to worship Him. Many times, I didn't know what else to pray but, "My Jesus... My Jesus... My Jesus," as I poured out my hungry love for Him in tears and sobs. Those words pouring out of my yearning heart must have touched Jesus so deeply that He needed me to know just how much it moved Him. I had actually melted His heart, and He needed to give me a response. He repeated it back from His heart into mine. "My Jesse...My Jesse...My Jesse." He was extravagant in how He went out of His way to reveal this to me.

After a period of time in this ecstatic love-abduction-from-another-world, Jesus and His holy angels warped through that portal, ascending back to the celestial throne room. The ceiling closed back up and the brooding glory of the Holy Spirit lifted. My body woke up in what felt like a drunken stupor. I was sad that the encounter ended, yet exhilarated with the awe of what had just happened. I looked at the television set and the credits for *Leap of Faith* were rolling at the end. Somehow I doubt I missed much. All of a sudden, everyone began waking up from their slumber. God's sleeping gas must have evaporated. I told them what had just happened to me. They didn't have any idea what was going on, but David said he could feel that something was happening in the atmosphere.

We don't always know just how much our worship is affecting the heart of our Lord. I want to tell you that it surely does move Him beyond your wildest imagination. Let it be known, He is touched by your worship, and He is responding.

Sweeter Than Wine, Part 2

It is very important to God that we discover His heart for us. He wants us to know how much He adores us and yearns for us. Check out some of these snippets of His love poetry for us. The following are more lyrics from the Song of Solomon. This time, instead of it being about how much we need Him, it is Jesus serenading us.

How beautiful you are, my darling, how beautiful you are! Your eyes are like doves behind your veil; your hair is like a flock of goats that have descended from Mount Gilead (Song of Solomon 4:1).

I don't quite grasp the flattery in comparing your hair with a flock of goats. But apparently, He is fond of your do. More importantly though, is to understand that He thinks you are absolutely beautiful and adorable. When He looks into the depths of your eyes, He sees doves. He loves the fact that He sees the Holy Spirit staring back at Him right through the windows of your soul.

Your teeth are like a flock of newly shorn ewes which have come up from their washing, all of which bear twins, and not one among them has lost her young. Your lips are like a scarlet thread, and your mouth is lovely. Your temples are like a slice of a pomegranate behind your veil. Your neck is like the tower of David, built with rows of stones on which are hung a thousand shields, all the round shields of the mighty men (Song of Solomon 4:2-4).

In modern western culture, we may not quite understand how all of these phrases could melt a heart. My teeth are like a flock of sheep? Well, gee, thanks. Baaaaaa. The sides of my forehead look like the inside of pomegranates? Yuk.

Of course this is not at all the heart of what the Beloved is saying to his bride. On the contrary, He is speaking love poetry through Solomon's creative words, words that meant something special to his wife to paint a picture of how much he adored her. The language made a lot more sense to them in their time and culture.

This is a picture of how Jesus sees you. He inspects every part of who you are. Don't forget, you are fearfully and wonderfully made (Psalm 139:14). He is looking you over from the inside out, and all He sees is beauty. If you could hear the words that He is speaking over you, they are words that would mean something deep to you personally, words that would melt your heart. What is He speaking over you?

Please do not hear this in a wrong way that could sound sacrilegious, but in a sense, Jesus practically worships you as His lover. He is head over heels for you! As He inspects you, He thinks such thoughts as, *"Your mouth is lovely."* Only a person who is in love will say something like that. You are absolutely gorgeous in His sight. He sums all of His words of adoration up in saying, *"You are altogether beautiful, my darling, and there is no blemish in you"* (Song of Solomon 4:7).

When He inspects you, He is doing it from love. Through the lens of love, all things are beautiful. He says that there is no blemish in you. When you see someone by true love, you do not retain a record of wrongs (see 1 Corinthians 13:5). God doesn't even see the imperfections. Love makes all things beautiful. You are beautiful to Him, blemish-free. *"Just as He chose us in Him before the foundation of the world, that we would be holy and blameless before Him"* (Ephesians

1:4). This is the way He views you and me who are in Christ. "... *Love covers a multitude of sins*" (1 Peter 4:8).

When you are head over heels in love with someone, you just cannot focus on their flaws. This is Jesus. This is you. Beauty is in the eye of the beholder, and He is beholding you. He is wearing rose-colored glasses, and you are the object of His obsession!

You have ravished my heart, my sister, my spouse; you have ravished my heart with one look of your eyes, with one link of your necklace (Song of Solomon 4:9 NKJV).

The Beloved is telling his wife that she has ravished his heart. Even with one glance of her eyes, his heart is ravished. *Ravish* means "to hold spellbound; to overwhelm with emotions, to seize, to carry off with force." Jesus is telling you that your love towards Him has seized His heart and taken it into custody, making Him spellbound by your expressions of love. On His end of the equation, when you set your affections on Him in adoration, you *katalambano* (apprehend) His heart and draw Him in, whether you know it or not.

How fair is your love, my sister, my spouse! How much better than wine is your love, and the scent of your perfumes than all spices! (Song of Solomon 4:10 NKJV).

Whoah! We need to stop and have a *Selah* moment.

Jesus is telling you that your love is better than wine! This verse is His response to us when we express to Him that His love is better than wine (see Song of Solomon 1:2). He is trying to give us a clue into His own personal experience in this love encounter. The same way that we get overwhelmed in the euphoria of His love for us, He also has the same experience by our love for Him.

Jesus Christ, believe it or not, gets intoxicated on our love for Him. When we *katalambano* His love, He is absolutely smitten. He can't help Himself. I actually believe that many of the times when we feel the ecstasies of His love, it is simply just a spillover of His own personal experience. It is not just us having an encounter with God. God is having an encounter with us! The bliss goes two ways. It takes two to tango.

We may love to worship the Lord through singing praises and dancing to express our love for Him with every bit of our heart and strength. But do we realize that He is the one who is leading the dance? *"The Lord your God is in your midst, a victorious warrior. He will exult* (Hebrew: *Sus-* **"rejoice"**) *over you with **joy**, He will be quiet in His **love**, He will **rejoice*** (Hebrew: *Gheel-* "spin around violently in joy"; in other words, He will dance up a party) *over you with shouts of **joy*** (Zepheniah 3:17). That is a lot of joyful expressions of love over you. Jesus is crazy about you! He is absolutely drunk on love with you. He is the One saying, "I'm in love! I'm in love! and I don't care who knows it!" He shouts it from the rooftops so all will know. You light up His soul!

Love Is Better Than Olive Oil

Have you ever played the flower petal game that supposedly helps to discern if the person you secretly love shares the same feelings? It is where you take a daisy and peel off a petal saying, "She loves me!" Then you peel the next one off and say, "She loves me not." You keep doing this until you get to the very last one. Superstition believes that whatever statement is said when the last petal is pulled is how she feels about you.

I remember a scene in a movie I liked when I was four or five years old called *Popeye* (with Robin Williams). Before Olive Oyl ever discovered that she loved Popeye, she was in a relationship with his soon-to-be foe, Bluto. Her house was full of family and friends as they awaited Bluto's arrival for an engagement party…for their fourth engagement. He was a big, strong, and mean man. With glaring eyes and furled brows, he growled past the crowd carrying a pink daisy. Olive was upstairs with her friends seemingly getting ready for the party.

Bluto began playing the "she loves me, she loves me not" game as he walked around the room intimidating each person. He pulled the first petal off the flower saying, "She **loves** me!" Everyone nervously cheered. He kept going. "She **don't** love me." Everyone was sad and anxious. "She'll marry me!" he said with the next yank. Everyone cheered again. "She won't marry me." Each time he got to the negative one, he either hurt someone or threatened to. About this time, Olive Oyl had sneaked out the upstairs window to run away from this dire situation.

Again he plucked the next petal. "She will!" Everyone celebrated, including a man he smashed to the floor like an accordion. He went for the next one. "She…" He paused and snarled as he looked at the flower. There was only one petal remaining, and he remembered where it was heading. Unfortunately, he had just walked up to Olive's unlucky brother, Castor Oyl.

Before he could cock his fist, Olive's girlfriends had just interrupted the party to tell Bluto that she was missing. They kept stuttering in fear until he demanded that they spit it out. They chickened out and said she was still getting ready. He said, "Good!" and then asked Castor, "Now where were we?" Castor was a clever man. He cunningly reminded him where he left off with the last one, but said the opposite. "She won't marry you; she…" and left it for Bluto to complete. "She **will**!" Bluto said with excitement as he plucked the final daisy petal. Everyone cheered with great relief. Castor got away by the skin of his teeth and a near faint.

Thankfully, we do not have to go through this kind of turmoil to find out if God is in love with us or not. With God, the daisy has only one petal. There is no alternative. "He loves me!" And that's all there is to it. There is no doubt about it; Jesus is busting at the seams with love for you!

22

Simply Unconditional

would like for you to hear a story about a friend of mine (anonymous at his request) who carries a strong revelation of this unconditional love of God and lives to share it with anyone who hungers for it. I appreciate his pure heart for God and for people. In his own words:

> Today at the gas station, I was approached by a young girl who promptly asked me, "How much?" I gave her a confused look and replied, "For what?" She then winked at me and said, "For me." I laughed and told her that she has already been paid for. This time she gave *me* the confused look. So then I introduced her to Jesus. She came expecting to make a few bucks; little did she know that she would inherit a Kingdom.

Now if that isn't a story of the radical, extravagant love of God, I don't know of any. God is thrilled to express His heart upon anyone who will receive it, regardless of their lifestyle or current condition. He is so lavish that He is giving His Kingdom to sinners if they will only receive it by faith. If He would do this for a sinner, what would He give to His children? There is nothing that can cause us to miss out on the glorious, intimate union with God and His infinite love...nothing except our own decision to doubt it or reject it.

For I am convinced that neither death, nor life, nor angels, nor principalities, nor things present, nor things to come, nor powers, nor height, nor depth, nor any other created thing, will be able to separate us from the love of God, which is in Christ Jesus our Lord (Romans 8:38-39).

Amor Vincit Omnia

Amor Vincit Omnia. This is Latin for "Love Conquers All Things." It is a phrase that was written by the Roman poet Virgil in *The Eclogues* a few decades before Christ arrived. He said, "Love conquers all things; so we too should yield to love."

Love isn't a condition; it is a Person. If we will surrender ourselves to the God of Love (and I am not referring to Eros or Aphrodite), we will be filled with His love and thus be able to conquer all things that used to overpower us. Virgil was ahead of his time when he captured a truth that Paul would be expounding on in the not-too-distant future as he brought Jesus into it. To echo it again, "*In all these things we overwhelmingly conquer through Him who loved us*" (Romans 8:37).

Do you remember my hero, Catie, from chapter 1? The formerly depressed and suicidal young lady who was miraculously healed of 150 scars that she had cut into her forearms from her previous life? Her story doesn't end with her fresh, smooth, feminine arms. That is where her story actually begins.

"At first I didn't believe it. Scars can't go away. But all the guilt and the pain, the years of torment and the shame, they all went away with the scars," she said. "This was the first time I felt like all the excuses for why God couldn't love me were completely eliminated." When Catie experienced the miraculous, lavish grace of Christ that day, the most important transformation wasn't in her flesh, but in her heart. Hope was born in her life like she had never known.

She recalled something said to her by the pastor who led her to Jesus nearly two years before this miracle. "Whoever has the most hope has the most influence." She didn't understand what that meant at the time, but she soon began to see it unfold. Since then, she has changed so much that she cannot recognize herself from who she was even a year ago. In the past, when she saw people going through the same problems she suffered, she would hopelessly say, "Good luck," and carry on with her own depression. But now she is able to see them with hope-filled compassion. "Now I genuinely love people, not just because it is the Christian thing to do." Catie has been finding many ways to reach out to the broken.

The unconditional love of God has radically transformed Catie so much that she is finding herself with a supernatural courage like she never knew. She used to live in great fear and intimidation. One of her greatest fears was to speak in front of crowds of people. God began to work on that one immediately. When the leaders of the conference she was attending learned of her miracle, they brought her to the stage so she could testify of God's goodness in front of several hundred people. Yes, she was nervous. But love drove her to push past her fear so she could honor the Lord publicly.

There is no fear in love; but perfect love casts out fear (1 John 4:18).

Catie decided that she would not let her fears control her any longer. She began a journey that day of choosing love over fear. Love fills us with a power to rise up in courage and face our giants so we can conquer them.

Nelson Mandela said, "I learned that courage was not the absence of fear, but the triumph over it. The brave man is not he who does not feel afraid, but he who conquers that fear."

Eleanor Roosevelt said, "You gain strength, courage, and confidence by every experience in which you really stop to look fear in the face. You are able to say to yourself, 'I lived through this horror. I can take the next thing that comes along.'"

Catie decided she wasn't a victim anymore. She began to search for opportunities to step out and take risks in her newfound love for Christ. The very next month, she was invited to go on an outreach ministry trip to Chicago. The trip was led by a good friend of mine, Elizabeth Reisinger, who had also been mentoring and loving on Catie for several months.

This was her first ministry adventure and she was extremely intimidated. She followed the team like a lost puppy, not knowing what she was doing. But Elizabeth's team coached her in how to pray for the sick, and they were getting healed. Her faith began to increase. They even went into a hospital to pray for patients. She realized that God can use anybody to heal. The next day, they went into downtown Chicago. She prayed for a man with excruciating, unbearable back pain. He was completely healed.

This was Catie, the former "not good enough" Catie. But that's not who she is any longer. No, this is the "Princess" Catie, daughter of the Most High God, laying hands on the sick. The man said this was the first time he had ever felt loved. Catie knew that she was now activated for healing and boldness.

God was so proud of Catie for her courageous love, a love which pursued greater freedom in the fullness of God. He was so pleased with her process that He decided to take it to another level. While in Chicago, He spoke to her in a dream. She dreamed that she was on a stage in the limelight preaching the gospel to thousands of people and God was moving through her in power. When she woke up, she was nervous because public speaking is among her greatest fears. She knew she couldn't hide from it, so she shared it with Elizabeth and me. However, hidden within that fear was an unusual excitement about where God wanted to take her in the future.

Her sense of time was different than God's. Graduation was less than one month away. Graduation was a big deal for Catie because she was twenty-two years old. This was another giant she finally decided to conquer. Because of all the traumatic losses to overdose and suicide that Catie had to grieve, she dropped out of high school three different times, each within three weeks of graduation. She says she wasn't afraid of failing, but of succeeding. But now she was living a new life, and she wanted to complete what she started. She was ready to get closure. She tackled this obstacle and conquered it. Graduation was finally here.

Catie barely wanted to walk to the front to receive her diploma in front of an audience, let alone speak. Yes, I did just say "speak." She was actually invited to give the graduation speech for her class. She was scared. But she had a new love in her which caused a new courage to swell up within her. Catie spoke to the assembly about her mom, about being bullied throughout life, and about how she chose to walk through pain even though it's difficult.

She was nervous because she thought that everyone would think she was weird. However, as she looked throughout the crowd, everyone was bawling their eyes out. After the ceremony, many people came up to her so they could tell her how amazing she was. Even the superintendent, who was not known as the complimentary type, shook her hand and said it was the most amazing graduation speech she had ever heard. (She had heard over 200.) Catie realized that she can speak in front of crowds without letting fear intimidate her.

Not long after graduation, Catie's friend's brother committed suicide. She felt deep pain as she mourned this latest loss; but she noticed that, in her mourning, there was hope this time. His family asked if she would speak at his funeral. She remembered her dream in Chicago. God was setting her up sooner than she had suspected. Request granted.

As she timidly stood there, looking upon hundreds of grieving family members and friends of the deceased boy, the grace of the Lord came upon her and brought her strength. She began to share her life testimony of God's extravagant love. The more she spoke, the stronger she felt. She taught them, "You can't walk through hard things without hope in God's love." Her message released supernatural hope on the listening audience, and over 100 people were saved that day!

Within a few months' time, Catie was invited to speak at five different funerals so she could release her story of hope upon the brokenhearted. One of the funerals was for a 14-year-old girl whom she had nannied for years. It was yet another suicide. Catie's heart was thrashed. It took everything she had to scrounge up the strength to speak at this gut-wrenching funeral, let alone just to make it through the day. The girl's mother asked Catie to not tell her daughter's story but her own story. There were so many children present who were friends of this deceased girl. After Catie returned home in distress, she received around 70 emails from kids who wanted to give up, but they now had new hope. Catie had shown them that there is a way out. Catie said, "It makes every ounce of pain worth it."

Soon after this, she was again invited to speak in public. This one, thankfully, was not for a funeral. It was for a youth rally that she was told would be for 500 church kids. She accepted. Once she was there, she realized it was actually an outdoor evangelistic event in the ghetto of inner city Detroit. It was then when she learned that the kids were instructed to invite five friends to come. 500 turned into 1000.

When Catie was standing on the stage, leaning on crutches with a fractured ankle, she looked across the crowd and recognized people she used to party with. This began to feel extremely awkward. But love conquers all! She shared her life testimony of the radical love of God. Before she could even give an altar call, people began rushing forward. Four hundred and three people (that they know of) gave their lives to the Lord that day!

After she was finished speaking, she went into the crowd to pray for people. A large, 25-year-old man came up to her and asked her to pray for healing. He had a fresh bullet wound in his belly. She prayed for him. Then they both were instantly confused and began freaking out as they watched the open bullet hole close up, seal, and heal right in front of their eyes! "I didn't know this God is for real. I just came because a friend invited me," he confessed. He was not hesitant to give his life over to Jesus after that.

Then a 12-year-old girl asked if they could pray for an elderly lady. Because of the noise in the crowd, Catie wasn't able to hear what the prayer request was. So she prayed that the old woman would feel the love of God. Nothing extraordinary seemed to happen, so she moved on to pray for others. However, after she walked away, the woman began rejoicing because her left eye that was completely blind was completely healed! Catie was walking in accidental miracles that night.

One thing Catie has in common with God is that, once she discovered His love for her, she decided there are no other options. She has given Him a one-petal daisy. The stakes are the same with you and God. He has given you His one-petal daisy. He loves you, and that's just how it is. No other options. No plan B. Knowing His love, we can give Him a one-petal daisy, too. Our response to God can be with reckless abandon. It is worth every ounce of pain and every ounce of joy.

Conclusion

Catie is a beautiful example of what God's love will do for someone who is at rock bottom in brokenness and hopelessness. God loves you with the same fervor, the same tenacity, the same intensity. Whether you are at rock bottom, high in the sky, or floating somewhere in-between, He wants to lavish you with His unlimited, unconditional love. His love imparts identity to us; it convicts our hearts for righteousness; it empowers strength to live in freedom and righteousness; it invites us into outrageous love encounters with Himself.

God's love is unconditional. His grace is unearned. They are both limitless and both intertwined. Loving grace doesn't just get down in the gutter with us and accept us as is. It pumps us with divine strength to empower us to rise up and become more than conquerors. It doesn't simply excuse our weaknesses; it lifts us above our weaknesses and makes us strong enough to overcome them and live victoriously.

Loving grace doesn't simply create strong Christians; it creates partakers of a divine nature, children of the Most High God. It gives us courage to rise above our fears, for fear is the enemy of our future. "The dogs of doom stand at the doors of your destiny. When you hear them barking, you know you are near your promised land," – Kris Vallotton.

Perfect love casts out fear (1 John 4:18).

What can life look like for someone who is smitten by the love of Christ and driven by a love for Him? How will our lives be changed when we discover that God is enjoying this love affair more than we ever could? You are a love encounter waiting to happen! You truly are a manifestation of the love of God—His dream come true. Let His dream become your reality, seeing yourself wholly as He sees. God is love. You are loved. His love is simply unconditional, and you can do nothing about it!

Appendix:
Meet the Lover of Your Soul

The gospel has too often been preached with hellfire and brimstone as a method to scare people into heaven (or their churches). But *gospel* actually means "good news," not bad news. The good news is that God's heart for you is not to condemn and make you feel horrible about yourself; it is to rescue you from hell and the corruption of sin so you can enjoy abundant life—friendship with God. It is a way to enter into the joy of the Lord. God invites you to receive eternal life today!

The Problem

1 John 4:8 says, *"God is love."* In Genesis chapter 1, we see that God created mankind in His image and made all things good. He formed this world to host His love and created people to receive it. His greatest desire was to build a family on this earth with whom He could share His kingdom.

Genesis chapter 2 tells us that He entrusted the Garden of Eden to His first children, Adam and Eve, so they could rule it in pleasure. Being one with God, Adam and Eve were to bring forth the human race under the blessing of Heaven.

God only gave them one rule to obey—do not eat of the tree of the knowledge of good and evil (see Genesis 2:17 NKJV).

Unfortunately, the devil was also in the garden and tempted them to sin. When they obeyed his voice instead of God's, they ignorantly transferred their allegiance to a new lord, breaking heart-connection with God, the source of Life. This act of treason brought death upon themselves, first in spirit and later in body. (See Genesis chapter 3.)

The worst part of this is that they gave birth to the human race, not within God's Kingdom, but under the rulership of satan. John 10:10 says the devil came to steal, kill, and destroy. This insurmountable blunder caused the corruption we still experience in this world today.

> *Therefore, just as through one man* (Adam) *sin entered the world, and death through sin, and thus death spread to all men, because all sinned* (Romans 5:12 NKJV).

> *For the wages of sin is death, but the gift of God is eternal life in Christ Jesus our Lord* (Romans 6:23 NKJV).

The effect of sin is death and separation from God and His blessings. The greatest tragedy in history is mankind becoming separated from God. Because we all have sinned, we all deserve hell and eternal separation from God.

Wait a minute! I thought this was supposed to be good news. Well, that was the bad news first. The good news is…

The Solution

Jesus Christ became our substitute! Jesus is the Son of God and came to the earth as a sinless man. Our sins were so great that only God Himself could provide a sufficient sacrifice to cover them all. The penalty that was due for our sins was inflicted upon Jesus as He sacrificed His life for ours (see Isaiah 53:4-5). On the cross, Jesus appeased the wrath of God for the sins of humanity.

> *For He made Him who knew no sin to be sin for us, that we might become the righteousness of God in Him* (2 Corinthians 5:21 NKJV).

On the cross, Jesus took upon Himself all of the sins you and I have ever committed and ever will commit. As He was dying, He said, *"Father, forgive them, for they do not know what they do"* (Luke 23:34). We have been forgiven.

Jesus paid the wages and crucified our sins and sinful natures on the cross by dying for us. He didn't just bear our sins; He took them away completely. He was called *"the Lamb of God who takes away the sin of the world!"* (John 1:29).

On the third day after Jesus died, He rose back to life again from the grave. He is the Resurrection and the Life (see John 11:25), and in Him death cannot be found. In Christ, we are given the gift of eternal life through His resurrection. Jesus conquered the grave! He is powerful enough to conquer any problem in your life too.

Jesus became the one and only doorway back into the household of Papa God. He said, *"I am the way, and the truth, and the life; no one comes to the Father but through Me"* (John 14:6).

Salvation restores your relationship with God. As we read above in 2 Corinthians 5:21, Jesus makes you become the righteousness of God. In Christ, you can be made right with God!

So how can you receive this blessing?

The Invitation

For God so loved the world, that He gave His only begotten Son, that whoever believes in Him shall not perish, but have eternal life (John 3:16).

You are promised eternal life by believing in Jesus. This isn't simply referring to a belief that Jesus exists; it speaks of a faith that proactively connects the heart to Christ's reality. It is an act of embracing this truth with faith.

If you confess with your mouth the Lord Jesus and believe in your heart that God has raised Him from the dead, you will be saved. For with the heart one believes unto righteousness, and with the mouth confession is made unto salvation (Romans 10:9-10 NKJV).

To be saved, you must believe in your heart that Jesus was not only crucified for your sins, but that He was raised from the dead.

Furthermore, we are called to confess our faith with our mouths. *"Out of the abundance of the heart his mouth speaks"* (Luke 6:45 NKJV). It is important to profess out of our mouths what we believe in our heart. There is power in the confession of faith.

> *Whoever calls on the name of the LORD shall be saved* (Romans 10:13 NKJV).

It's time for you to become all you can be in Christ. If you wish to give your heart to Jesus and receive His free gift of salvation, please pray the following prayer aloud:

The Prayer

Dear Jesus, I believe You are the Son of God and that You came to the earth to die for my sins on the cross. I believe You rose from the dead and ascended to Heaven where You live now. I believe You are the only way to the Father. I want You to live in me!

I am a sinner. I ask You to forgive me of all my sins and cleanse me from them with Your blood. Remove their power from my life so I can be free to live completely for You.

From this day forward, I choose to follow You and live in relationship with You. I choose to live for You instead of myself or this world. I am Yours and I surrender all. Thank you that I am now born again and a child of the Most High God! Amen.

The Result

Now that you believe in your heart and have confessed with your mouth, it is time to celebrate! You just made the best decision of a lifetime. Jesus has broken the chains of sin off of you and cleansed you. You are free. Praise God!

Second Corinthians 5:17 says, *"Therefore, if anyone is in Christ, he is a new creation; old things have passed away; behold, all things have become new"* (NKJV).

Your sins and your old sinful nature have been crucified with Jesus (see Galatians 2:20). He has given you a new life IN CHRIST. You have been "born again" (see John 3:3-8).

God did not intend for Christianity to be about a list of dos and don'ts. It is all about enjoying a relationship with Him. It is a love encounter. God isn't expecting perfection. He's looking for you to love Him in response to His love for you. Through relationship, He will work His will into your heart so that you can begin to naturally live a life that pleases Him. In Christ, you now have the power to overcome sin and to live a joy-filled life of freedom.

Here are a few suggestions for really good ways to enhance your new relationship with God:

1. **Read your Bible daily.** This will help you understand how God thinks and feels about things. It will help your thoughts and feelings to become more like His.
2. **Pray and worship daily.** Don't pray a liturgy; be a friend. Share your heart and mind about all parts of life. He is your new Best Friend who cares. He wants to share His heart with you too.
3. **Do life with a group of Bible-believing Christians.** Christianity was never meant to be done alone. One important way we grow in our relationship with God is by practicing community with other believers who have dedicated their lives to a relationship with Jesus. We all build one another up in strength.

If you prayed this prayer to begin a new life with Jesus, I would love to celebrate with you. Please send me a message at fromtheoverflow.com/contact-us to share your good news. I bless your new journey in Christ! I am so excited for you!

Letter from Author

Dear beloved of God,

Thank you for reading this book! I hope you have been encountering the manifest love of God and are experiencing His radical grace.

If you feel this book would bless other people, I would highly appreciate your recommendation to them! Word-of-mouth is the most powerful form of marketing, and you can help us get this gospel message spread abroad to places it may never reach otherwise.

Please visit our website at www.fromtheoverflow.com to learn more about our ministry and, more importantly, to enjoy more of the message of God's goodness and His kingdom. We would love for you to sign up for a free subscription.

God bless,
Jesse Cupp

Please subscribe to www.fromtheoverflow.com for free!

I would love it if you would take a moment to give an honest rating for this book on your preferred online bookstore!

17683289R00135

Made in the USA
Middletown, DE
04 February 2015